Table Of Contents

Introduction

Chapter One: Your Ultimate Goals with Affiliate Marketing and as an Online Entrepreneur

Introduction
  Merchant
  Affiliates
  Customers
  Network

Goals
  Revenue
  Cost and Profitability
  Connection
  Endless Possibilities
  It is Convenient
  You can Track Your Progress
  Autonomy to Select the Products and Projects
  Work from Anywhere
  Steady Cash Flow

Chapter Two: The Beauty of Sales and Marketing

How to Sell Anything to Someone or Anyone?
  You are Selling Yourself
  Listen
  Know Who to Sell to
  Motivation
  Keep it Simple
  Business Benefits
  Opening and Closing Deals as an Affiliate Marketer and Entrepreneur
  Worth
  Negotiate the Process
  Benchmarks and Deadlines
  Discuss
  Ranges
  Negotiate

How to Market Yourself
  Your Niche
  Recognition
  Wisdom
  Community
  Social Media
  Soft Skills

Leadership
Teamwork
Communication
Problem-Solving
Flexibility
Time Management

Brand Positioning
Target Audience
Market
Promise
Reason

Chapter Three: People/Networking/Interpersonal Skills

Building Relations
Active Listening
Assertiveness
Communication
Self-Management

Chapter Four: Building Your Eco-System

Affiliate Websites
Amazon Associates
Cons
ShareASale Affiliates
eBay Partners
Cons
Shopify Affiliate Program
Clickbank
Pros
Rakuten Marketing Affiliates
Cons
Leadpages Partner Program
StudioPress Affiliate Website
Cons
CJ Affiliate Publisher's Program
Pros

Picking the Right Affiliate Program
Terms and Conditions
Avoid Paid-for Programs
Check the Business

Lead Magnets
Resource List
Quick-Start Guide
Cheat Sheet
Video Answer
Checklist
Email Scripts

Mini-Course
Book Chapter
Course Module
Quiz
Template
Transcript
Bonus Audio
Live Training

Team for Affiliate Marketing
Senior Strategist
Affiliate Manager
Data Analyst
Ad Operations

Whether You Need a Team or Not?

Social Media Marketing
Social Media Platforms to Use
How to Succeed with Social Media
Tips for Social Media Marketing Success

YouTube Videos
Setting It Up
Videos
A Good Thumbnail
Use Trends
Annotations
Promote On Other Channels
Captions
Miscellaneous

Chapter Five: Walking the Talk!

Dress to Kill, Impress to Kill & Nail Deals!
General Tips
Tips for Women
Tips for Men

Presentation Skills- 5-10 Minutes Deal
Defining the Problem
Describe the Solution Offered
Your Target Market
Describing Your Competition
Your Team
Financial Summary
Showing Traction with Milestones
How To Write Each Part
Identifying Your Goal
Explain What You Do
Communicating Your USP
Engaging with a Question

Putting it all Together
Practice
Additional Tips

Building Business Relationships
Be Authentic
Shared Values and Goals
Mutual Respect
Vulnerability
Loyalty
Meaningful Connection
Personal
Expectations
Sub-Affiliates

Chapter Six: Your Product

How to Select a Product/Service?
Make a List
Market Niche
Market

Start Affiliate Marketing
Find Your Niche
Research
Site Building
Making the Content
Reviews
Blogs on Current Affairs
Free Courses
Building an Audience
Social Media
Collaborations
Power of SEO
Email Lists
Paid Advertising
Promoting Affiliates
Product Reviews
Ads
Context Links
Email Promotion
Discounts and Giveaways
Repeat

Earn from Affiliate Marketing
Build Your Website Traffic First, and be Patient
Content is Very Important
Promote Your Site
Don't be Invisible or Anonymous

Chapter Seven: Creation of Digital/Informational Product

Step 1: Commitment

Step 2: Idea

Step 3: Test the Idea

Step 4: Create an Outline

Step 5: Course Content

Go Online

Conclusion

Resources

Chapter One: Your Ultimate Goals with Affiliate Marketing and as an Online Entrepreneur

Do you want to learn about affiliate marketing? Do you want to become a successful entrepreneur? But you aren't certain where to start? If your answer is yes to all these questions, then this is the perfect book for you. All the information about these topics that are available online these days can be quite overwhelming, especially for a beginner. You don't need to worry about this anymore; you have come to the right place.

Affiliate marketing is a phrase that you might have stumbled across online. There are tens of thousands of articles telling you why you must be minting money with affiliate marketing, and you might feel a little left out if your bank account isn't clocking up cash while you are sleeping. What exactly is affiliate marketing and how can you make use of it for generating a steady stream of passive income for yourself? To put it simply, affiliate marketing is the process of promoting or selling someone else's product or service. You earn a commission on any of the sales made or click through to a given affiliate site. Doesn't that sound quite simple? In theory, you can have a website without any products or services of your own. It can be a blog, an online journal, or anything similar to it. As long as there is some relation to the product or the service, you are set. Maintaining a website costs money and with affiliate marketing, you can cover all those costs and earn more money. It doesn't cost the owner anything to sign up for an affiliate program and the business owner doesn't have to pay anything until he makes a sale. So, it is a win-win situation for both parties involved.

In this book, you will learn all that you need to become a good affiliate marketer and entrepreneur. You will learn about affiliate marketing, the traits of a good entrapper, the ways in which you can start affiliate marketing, the right tools and platforms to use, and the steps to market your product effectively. Apart from this, you will learn the ways in which you can sell anything to anyone, the tips to close deals successfully, steps to develop good presentation skills, interpersonal skills, and all the other things that you need to become a successful entrepreneur.

If you are ready to learn all this and change your life, then all that we need to do is get started. So, let us start without further ado.

Introduction

If you are looking for high-traffic advertising space on the Internet, then you need affiliate marketing. Selling a product can be difficult, even more so when you aren't able to reach out to your target audience. At times, you need a different method to sell your products. Affiliate marketing is a simple concept where the vendor can sell their products or services with the help of an affiliate. The affiliate is responsible for marketing the products to potential customers and facilitates the sale. The vendor provides a monetary compensation for the services that the affiliate provides. The concept of affiliate marketing is the brainchild of William J Tobin, the founder of PC Flowers & Gifts. They used Prodigy network to increase their sales and, in turn, they paid Prodigy Network for the services they offered. You probably haven't realized it yet, but affiliate marketing is quite prevalent. The simplest form of affiliate marketing is the reviews that you find about any product or service on the Internet. Using the Internet for affiliate marketing is a quite common and popular practice these days.

Affiliate marketing refers to the process of product creation and marketing using third-party resources and sharing revenue with all the parties involved, according to their contribution. There are mainly four parties involved, which are as follows.

Merchant

Merchants are the creators of the products or the brand, the seller, the retailer, etc. who are trying to sell their products. They are the ones who create the product and look for people who can promote it for them. Some examples of merchants are Microsoft, Dyson, Phillips, etc. There might also be individuals involved who happen to be sole proprietors of their company. As long they have a product to sell, they will be the merchants.

Affiliates

Affiliates are known as the publishers. Affiliates can be individuals or companies who promote products and services that belong to merchants. So, if you are popular and have significant traffic, then you can be an affiliate. All you have to do is promote a product that belongs to the merchant and earn revenue by doing so. The business can be extremely lucrative, with people making anywhere from hundreds to thousands of dollars a month. The system is quite simple. If you help the merchant by diverting your traffic to their site and get some to buy the products, then you will make an income from the sale.

Customers

Customers are some of the most critical aspects of the system and the reason why the system can be kept alive. They are required to click on the links provided by the customers so that it leads to a sale and the revenue can be shared. Consumers usually look for links as they might find discounts and coupons waiting for them. Social network happens to be one of the easiest places to find discounts and codes. However, a majority of customers will not know that they are part of a marketing system and end up clicking and buying from third-party sites, thereby becoming a part of it without actively knowing about it.

This does not mean the consumer will end up paying more for products, as the cost of affiliation will be included in the cost of the product. The affiliate marketer will allow the affiliation to run in the background while the sale takes place without the knowledge of the customer.

Network

Although most affiliate marketers do not feel like they are part of a network, a network exists and includes affiliates and merchants. It is the link between the two and how they can find each other. These networks make it easier to promote affiliates and generate a steady flow of business. Many networks and websites provide this link and include the likes of Clickbank and ShareASale. These mostly handle the sale and promote the products. Some affiliates end up going through an affiliate program just to promote a product while some go through it to know about the database of the products to choose the right ones.

Goals

The popularity of affiliate marketing has increased along with the advances in technology, now marketers can attract a larger audience to websites that are full of different advertisements. Ambitious affiliate marketers are usually self-employed individuals with a set of goals and objectives that help them succeed. Before you decide to opt for affiliate marketing, you need to have specific goals in mind that you think affiliate marketing will help you achieve. In this section, you will learn about certain goals that you can consider.

Revenue

The goal of any marketing program is to earn revenue and the goal of affiliate marketing is the same. All affiliate marketers tend to set short-term as well as long-term objectives that continually push them to increase the value of the services they offer. There are different ways in which affiliate marketers can be paid. For instance, the payment can depend on the clicks per advertisement, paid per clicks that lead to a sale, or anything like this. So, the affiliate marketer gets paid only when the customer or the audience performs a particular action. The marketer tries to increase the instances of such happenings to increase their revenue and, in this manner, they also help the business increase their revenue. The goal of any entrepreneur is to increase their income and affiliate marketing helps meet this goal.

Cost and Profitability

Affiliate marketing uses a lean business model. It means that most of the operations can be usually managed from home and the business owner is the sole employee. The idea of keeping costs low is that the affiliate marketer can leverage this and reduce their overhead costs while increasing their revenue.

As an entrepreneur, you will always try to increase your profits, and you can do this with the help of affiliate marketing. When your costs are low, your profit margin will automatically increase. If cost reduction is your goal, then affiliate marketing will certainly help you achieve this goal.

Connection

If you think that you have a strong connection to a specific product, then you can bank on this connection and create a source of income for yourself. No one likes a pushy salesman. At times, it can be quite obvious when someone pushes others to believe in a product they don't believe in themselves. If you think you like a product and you know that you are a good salesperson, then affiliate marketing is the right way to go. Affiliate marketing helps you capitalize on this connection you have and connect to your audience with it.

Endless Possibilities

One of the quickest ways in which you can start a home-based company is by taking up affiliate marketing. There are no limitations on the amount of income you can earn from affiliate marketing and there is hardly any financial risk associated with signing up for affiliate programs.

It is Convenient

When you start affiliate marketing, you can work at your own convenience and you are in charge of setting up your own working hours. When you work for someone else, you will have to work when they tell you. There might be times when you have to extend your working hours to meet a deadline. However, with affiliate marketing, you can start working when you want to, and you can select working hours that will suit your lifestyle. Or you can select such hours in which you know that your body will be at the peak of its concentration.

You can Track Your Progress

You can easily check the numbers of your audiences or people you are reaching out to, the products you created and sold, and the profits you are making as well.

Autonomy to Select the Products and Projects

You don't have to worry about projects that don't interest you. You can start working on things that interest you and you don't have to take up those things that you aren't passionate about. You don't have to do something you don't really know or the things you do not want to work on.

Work from Anywhere

Since there is no fixed workplace or work hours, you can pretty much work from anywhere in the world that you want to as long as you have access to the Internet. You can carry your work along with you and work at your convenience.

Steady Cash Flow

One of the main advantages of affiliate marketing is the steady cash flow it generates. Although working for someone else will guarantee that you receive a paycheck at the end of every month, you have to do your job competently, go to work early, and do all the things that your employer asks you to do. However, the salary you receive is fixed, regardless of how well you perform. When you take up affiliate marketing, you can keep earning as long as you are successful at what you are doing and there is no limit on the money you can earn.

Chapter Two: The Beauty of Sales and Marketing

How to Sell Anything to Someone or Anyone?

You can sell anything to anyone, provided you know what you need to do. In this section, you will learn the different tips that you can use if you want to sell anything to anyone.

You are Selling Yourself

The first thing that you need to keep in mind when you opt for affiliate marketing is that you need to sell yourself to your public. Forget about the product or service you want to offer. If your audience doesn't like you, then they will not listen to you, regardless of how wonderful your product it. You not only need to present the product or service well, but you need to present yourself well too. Your audience will listen to you only if they like you. You need to be the kind of salesperson that you would want to buy things from.

Listen

An important skill that all good salespersons possess is that they are good listeners. A bad salesperson never stops talking about the product or service that they offer, and they tend to keep going on and on about it. Well, a good salesperson knows that it is important to listen to your audience. You need to learn to listen to their needs and then you can present yourself accordingly. You cannot be a good entrepreneur if you don't have the patience to listen to anyone. Affiliate marketing is all about being personable so that others will want to buy things you endorse.

Know Who to Sell to

If you want to sell a widget that costs about $50,000, then you need to make sure that you don't try to sell it to someone with a budget of $12000. You need to understand your audience and gauge whether you can sell to them or not. You cannot try to sell to an audience who has no use of what you are offering. You need to be realistic about your goals and need to keep in mind your audience as well. If you want to be a successful affiliate marketer, then you need to understand your audience. For instance, if your audience predominantly consists of fashion enthusiasts, then it is not a good idea to try selling a digital product about stock markets to them.

Motivation

Why must anyone care about what you are selling? How will your product or service add value to their life? You need to pay attention to what drives your potential customers in their life and whether you can address that need. Try to learn about the motivation that fuels your potential customers to purchase. If you can address that motivation, you can make it big as an affiliate marketer.

Keep it Simple

If you want to sell something to someone, then you need to keep your sales pitch quite simple. If you want them to take a specific action, like click on a link, then that's what your sales pitch needs to be about. Don't add unnecessary information and confuse your audience. It is a good thing that you want to seem knowledgeable, but if you overwhelm your audience with a lot of information, it will backfire. If you want to be a good affiliate marketer, then you always need to have a good elevator pitch handy. You will learn more about improving your presentation skills in the coming chapters.

Business Benefits

If you want to be able to sell anything to anyone, then you need to be fully aware of all that you offer and the purpose it serves. If you shift your mindset from selling to helping others, you can become a good salesperson. You need to be able to list all the benefits and value-added features you believe will help your audience at the drop of a hat.

Opening and Closing Deals as an Affiliate Marketer and

Entrepreneur

If you want to be a good entrepreneur, then you need to open and close deals. It doesn't matter how well you network with others if you cannot close deals. At the end of the day, your bottom line depends on all the deals you finalize. Without any deals, you cannot achieve the professional success that you want.

Worth

If you want to understand if a deal will be beneficial for you or not, then you need to be perfectly aware of who you are dealing with. It means that you need to know about their financial situation, the way they earn their keep, and how they spend it. You might think that these are just numbers. Well, remember that these numbers are critical when you need to close a deal. It is important that you know about the other party's financials and their budget. Start with the simple reason as to why a particular deal will make sense to your prospect. Once you are aware of their biggest problem, then you need to come up with your best solution to solve that problem. Business owners need to be careful when they do their research. Never rely solely on second-hand information and what others seem to think. You can take all of this into consideration when you need to make a decision, but they must not be the sole factor. You need to do your own research, understand the numbers, their implication, and what they mean to you.

Negotiate the Process

Before you discuss a specific issue, you need to discuss how the negotiation will proceed. What are the ground rules and who will facilitate the negotiation? What are the issues you want to discuss and when? You need to map out the process of negotiation so that it prevents you from making false assumptions and helps streamline your negotiations.

Benchmarks and Deadlines

You need to set a couple of short-term benchmarks and a couple of realistic as well as ambitious deadlines. What will happen if you don't meet a benchmark or deadline? You need to discuss a schedule and stick to it. Negotiations need to be timebound. In fact, this helps to increase creative thinking.

Discuss

Money matters tend to make a lot of people uncomfortable. In fact, a lot of people have trouble discussing money. You need to make sure that you are comfortable talking about money from the beginning. As an entrepreneur, you need to be clear about the money from the very beginning and don't waste your time or theirs by not talking about it. At the end of the day, every business is about making money. If you are uncomfortable talking about it, you will find yourself in a world of trouble.

Ranges

Whenever you need to speak in monetary terms, you need to use ranges of price, cost structure, yield and performance so that you can understand the highest and the lowest numbers that both parties can accommodate. If you don't do this, then you might find yourself in a situation where you cannot gauge whether the deal is worth all the trouble or not. Numbers are very important, and business is all about numbers.

Negotiate

You must always work on one specific aspect of the deal at any point before you move onto the next. You need to take it one thing at a time and don't try to tackle the entire deal at once. You must never negotiate before you fully understand all the details involved. Never negotiate before you get to this point. If you negotiate before this, then you might end up making a bad deal.

How to Market Yourself

You need to be able to market yourself well if you want to become a successful entrepreneur. If you want to be a good affiliate marketer, then you need to be able to market yourself. You need to give others a reason why they need to associate themselves with you.

Your Niche

The first step to marketing yourself is to understand your interests, talents, and passions. You need to think about different ways in which you can combine all these elements. Focus on all the uncommon things that you can offer others.

Recognition

You not only need to be knowledgeable about your niche, but you also need to know the manner in which you can showcase this knowledge. The best way to showcase all that you know is by developing a knowledge base. You need to ensure that your reputation grows, and you need to promote your opinions. Make sure that your opinions are well-informed and verifiable. You need to seek recognition for your expertise. You can do this by building and developing relationships with thought leaders and media reps in your community or niche.

Wisdom

The best way to market yourself is to write about what you know so that you can get your name in the public domain as an expert. You can contribute blog posts, articles, or anything that will make you seem like an expert. You need to make sure that the content you decide to share is informative, well-written and timely, and will add value to your readers.

Community

You need to develop a network of like-minded people in your field of work and get to know them. You need to build a community. You can offer genuine expertise and it will make your audience curious about you.

Social Media

Spend some time on social media. Social media is the ideal platform to market yourself. You can offer your expertise on these platforms for free and help build a fan base. The bigger your following, the better it is.

You need to remember that everything you do, everything you communicate, and every word that you say is a message to the audience. Remember that who you are is the message that you are sending the world.

Soft Skills

Soft skills are extremely important in today's world. These skills are intangible, and they refer to the skills that are all about your attitude, beliefs, intuition, and your ability to communicate with others. Soft skills are important because they allow you to share your ideas, connect with others, form partnerships, and help you move ahead in life. As an entrepreneur, soft skills are critical for your growth. So, you must be aware of all the soft skills you possess. Here is a list of all the soft skills that an entrepreneur must have.

Leadership

If you want to be an entrepreneur, then you need to be a good leader. You need to be able to influence and motivate others. The key to affiliate marketing is influencing others to take the action that you want them to. To become a good leader, you need to identify what people want and you need to be able to give it to them. So. If you think leadership is one of the soft skills you possess, then you need to work on honing it.

Teamwork

If you want to be successful as an entrepreneur, then you need to work well with others. Effective teamwork is essential to excel in life. You must not only be able to influence others, but you need to work well with them as well. As an affiliate marketer, collaborations with others are an important part of the job description. Social media is all about working with others. So, you need to be a good team player.

Communication

There are different forms of media that communication includes. For best results, you need to develop various communication skills. The essential communication skills are listening, writing, presentation, and speaking. You need all these skills to share your message with others. Your goal will merely stay a goal if you cannot communicate about it with others. When others understand what you are trying to communicate, it is more likely that they will understand your goal.

Problem-Solving

Problems will naturally come your way. You cannot avoid all problems and obstacles. Therefore, it is important that you can solve problems effectively. You need to be able to readily solve any problems that come your way. You need a good set of analytical skills as well as creativity to tackle a given situation. Apart from this, you need to be able to think differently and even come up with out-of-the-box solutions to overcome any hurdles you face. It is a critical soft skill for any entrepreneur.

Flexibility

Can you change direction and learn things easily? Flexibility is one of those skills that will help you survive as an entrepreneur in this ever-changing world. If you want to move ahead in life, then you need to change constantly and also keep up with all the changes taking place in the world. If you notice that something isn't working, then you need to be flexible and try a different option. An agile mind and a dynamic thought process are necessary to move ahead in life.

Time Management

Time is a finite resource and you need to know the best way to utilize it. If you want to succeed in life, then you need to be able to manage your time successfully. You need to be able to prioritize your tasks and differentiate between those things that you need to attend to immediately and all that you can do later.

Well, these are all the essential soft skills that you need to succeed in life. How many of these things do you possess? The good news is that it is quite easy to develop these soft skills. If you think that you already possess these skills, then the next step is to optimize them.

Brand Positioning

As an online entrepreneur, you need to concentrate on strategic positioning. In this section, you will learn about strategic positioning and the different methods you can use for strategic positioning. Strategic positioning is an important part of all the planning that goes into marketing a brand or a product. The process of deciding your strategic positioning starts when you define the value proposition your brand offers. It is a primarily customer-focused statement.

There are a couple of fundamental aspects that you need to be able to define if you want to work on strategic positioning. You need to know what you or your brand stands for. The objective you wish to fulfill (not a commercial objective). How can you provide value to your customers? Your answers to these questions will help you develop your mission statement.

If you want to work on your brand's strategic position, then you need to come up with a strategy that can bridge the gap between your value proposition and the wants of the audience. The idea of strategic positioning is to motivate your audience to act favorably towards your brand. For instance, let us assume that your mission statement is "We deliver exotic flowers to your home," and your market research shows that there is a demand for this particular service in your target audience, then your strategic position can be "Flowers from US's best independent florists, delivered to your doorstep." This is certainly an oversimplification, but it does show the logic used in strategic positioning.

Your strategic position is the combination of your mission statement and the data-driven strategic insight.

You need to use digital insights to improve your strategic positioning. A blue-chip company, a startup, or anyone can access vast quantities of data that can give you insights about your brand, your audience, and its online activity. You can use different analytic tools to view your statistics about your brand engagement on different social media platforms. For instance, you can use Google Analytics to learn about the visitors your website has and how each page of your website stacks up according to different performance metrics.

You need to make a list of all the things that you wish to know to help you decide on your brand positioning. For instance, you might want to know if a specific demographic likes product type A or B? Is the public opinion receptive to your product? Does your audience want a digital output for any of your products? If there is data that can be useful to you, then there is a means of finding it as well. The digitized world is your oyster and you can find all the data that you want through one means or the other. You need to continually review and add insights that you can use to align your strategic positioning. You need to remember that the world is dynamic and if you want to come out on top, then you need to keep up with it. Remember the three questions you had to answer to define your brand positioning? "Do you know what you or your brand stands for? What is the objective you wish to fulfill (not a commercial objective)? How can you provide value to your customers?" Reconsider these questions and relist your answers. With the answers to these questions along with any other key commercial objective that you used to define your strategic position, you will be able to list your strategic positioning factors. Now, you need to randomly select a couple of examples of your B2C communications and it can include videos, blog posts, any posts on social media, pretty much anything that you provide your audience, and you need to consider whether the message you want to convey is in sync with all the other factors on your list. If you think they aren't in sync, then you need to take the necessary steps to ensure positive action.

Well, why do you need to worry about strategic positioning? If you want to succeed as an entrepreneur, then you need to make sure that you have strong foundations to support your success. Strategic positioning helps improve your online and offline presence. A strategic position helps you to achieve a consistency between your brand's activity and tone of voice. It will encourage customers to not just trust but even invest in your brand. It helps to match your brand or the services you offer to a gap that exists in the market. It also creates a sense of purpose to work towards. It differentiates you from your competitors and helps you think about your brand strategy. Apart from all this, it also encourages customers to engage with the brand on a personal level. Did you know that strategic positioning helps with digital marketing? Yes, it does. Do you want to learn how strategic positioning helps with digital marketing? Then read on.

Well, you now know how digital insights make their way into the process of strategic positioning, the next step is to learn about how strategic positioning can help with your brand's online activity. Usually, customers progress through a sales funnel. A popular instance is when a customer starts to browse for a product or service with a vague notion of making a purchase. Then the customer moves onto an active state of interest in which they try to pursue a likely purchase. Once they make up their mind, that is when they reach checkout, they reach the stage of making a purchase. Once the customer makes a purchase, they enter a loyalty phase, which tends to modify the way they browse and, hopefully, the cycle will repeat. At each of these stages, you can use different forms of digital as well as non-digital means of communication to present different attributes of the strategic positioning of a brand. In each case, a specific aspect of the brand will appeal to the user, enabling them to move ahead in the sales funnel.

For instance, if a user is present in the browsing phase, then you can provide them with content that highlights your range in a simple format. You can use the data from their previous browsing sessions to identify the products or any other listicle that can serve them better. For instance, if a user visits your site and browses through a couple of pages on golfing equipment, then you can provide them content with articles like "The best Golf Clubs of 2018." The behavior of the user demonstrates their desire to browse through pages of golf products, and if you present them with targeted marketing, it can facilitate their objective. This is an example of digital strategic positioning in motion.

After this phase comes the phase of active interest. You can understand this from different behavioral triggers like repeatedly viewing a specific product page, the time spent on the site, and the list of items added to their cart. In this phase, your brand is actively building its case and it is all about convincing the customer to make a purchase. At this stage, your aim is to reinforce your brand's message to motivate the customer to make a purchase. You provided them with relevant content and now it is time to deepen your customer's interest.

There are different ways in which you can deal with the active phase. The idea is to drive the customer to make a purchase and close the sale. The best way to do this is to opt for a no-nonsense approach and reinforce your brand's strategic positioning.

Brand positioning is about positioning the brand in the mind of your potential customers. It is also known as the positioning strategy, brand positioning statement, as well as brand strategy. The goal of brand positioning is to create an impression in your customer's mind so that the customer associates your brand with something that is specific and desirable. It also helps distinguish your brand from others in the marketplace. It is a methodical system to find a window in the mind and is based on the concept that communication is desirable when it takes place at the right time and under the right circumstances.

Brand positioning statements are usually confused with taglines or slogans. A positioning statement is for internal use and these statements guide the marketing decisions. A positioning statement helps the entrepreneur make certain key decisions that will affect the perception of your audience about your brand. On the other hand, a tagline is a statement that is used in a marketing statement, and it is an external statement. Any insight from your positioning statement can be turned into a tagline.

If you want to create a positioning strategy, then you need to identify what makes your brand unique and differentiates it from your competitors. There are seven simple steps that you can use to clarify your positioning in the market.

You need to determine how your brand is positioning itself at present.

Then you need to identify your direct competition.

Understand the way in which each of your competitors is positioning themselves.

Compare the positioning of your brand with that of your competitors. It will help you identify what makes you unique.

Develop a distinct positioning idea.

Test the efficiency of your brand's positioning statement.

The brand positioning statement consists of a sentence or two that communicate the uniqueness of your brand and the value it offers customers compared to your competition.

A simple way to formulate your positioning statement is as follows:

For (your target audience) who (the opportunity you provide), the (name of the product or the service) is a (category of the product) that (state a key benefit or provide a compelling reason). Unlike (your primary competitor), our product or service (state the primary distinguishing factor). If you want to create a brand positioning statement, then here are a couple of simple things that you need to understand.

Target Audience

Who is your target audience? Who do you want your brand to appeal to? In general, what demographic description do you want to target? Who is your target audience and whom do you want your brand to attract?

Market

What is your ideal market? In which category is your brand competing and what is the relevance of your brand to your target audience?

Promise

What is the benefit that your brand can offer to your target audience? What is the emotional or rational benefit that your brand offers in relation to your competition?

Reason

What is the evidence that establishes that your brand delivers on its promise? You need some compelling evidence.

Take some time and answer these questions carefully. Once you have all your answers in place, you can develop your positioning statement. Your positioning statement will be as follows:

For (your target audience), (brand's name or company's name) is the (market definition) that delivers (the brand's promise) because only (your company's or brand's name) is the (reason to believe).

When you develop your brand positioning, here are a couple of criteria that it must meet.

Does the brand positioning differentiate your brand from that of your competitors?

Does it match the customer's perception of your brand?

Is it conducive of growth?

Does it clearly identify the unique value it offers to your target audience?

Does it help form a clear image in your mind that is different from that of your competition?

Does it focus on your core audience?

Is it memorable?

Is it consistent in all aspects of your business?

Is it easy to comprehend and is it difficult to copy?

Will it help with long-term success?

Does it make your brand seem credible and believable?

Will it be able to withstand any counterattack from your competition in the market?

Will it make your marketing strategy more effective?

If you can positively answer all these questions, then you have an effective brand positioning statement.

Chapter Three: People/Networking/Interpersonal Skills

At times, being an entrepreneur might feel like you need to balance ten dinner plates on ten sticks without letting any of the plates fall. It takes a lot of consistency as well as concentration to do it perfectly. There are different skills that an entrepreneur needs to master to become successful. These skills include managing marketing, sales, finance, accounts, leadership, management, and many other things. Even if you excel in all these skills, if you are a poor communicator then you will run into a lot of trouble. Poor communication is like a plate falling; it can ruin your entire performance. In fact, one of the most underrated skills is networking. You need interpersonal skills to network with others. If you want to grow as an entrepreneur, then you need to work on your interpersonal skills.

If you want to get things done and achieve all the goals you have set for yourself, then you need to work hard to establish good relationships with the people around you or all those you meet on your path. Here are a couple of interpersonal skills that you need to master.

Effective communication is possible only when you are a good speaker as well as listener. These two skills are necessary to establish a good working relationship with your customers, target audience, and others you collaborate with. You need to be a good listener, maintain eye contact, and ask questions to make sure that you are fully understood and also to make sure that the other person understands you as well. You also need to be able to communicate your ideas and plans, as well as expectations in a simple and precise manner so that everyone understands you. Good communication skills, both verbal as well as non-verbal, are necessary to improve your productivity.

In this fast-paced world that we live in, with all the advancements in technology, meeting people in person isn't the only way in which you meet new people. It is quite common to contact people via emails or even video calls. Good manners, as well as etiquette, are essential for a business interaction with associates and strangers alike. There are a couple of things that you must consider regardless of the form of communication. You must always be punctual, be well-dressed, listen carefully, empathize, don't be rude, don't interrupt when someone is talking, show interest in what the other is saying, and always be respectful. Good manners go a long way towards building a relationship.

Interpersonal skills are important for any entrepreneur because their basic job description involves communicating, interacting, and selling things to others. The ability to converse effectively with others is the backbone of networking. If you are good at networking, it will set you apart from your competitors. Apart from having the necessary physical and technical skills to do your job, an entrepreneur also needs to possess good interpersonal skills to negotiate well, close deals, and convey abstract ideas. Here are some interpersonal skills that an entrepreneur must possess.

Building Relations

If you want your business to grow, then you need to be able to attract more customers and retain your existing ones. Well, it might sound quite straightforward, but it isn't always easy. If you want to run a successful business, then you need to build and maintain relations. To build relations, you need to build trust, give and receive feedback, and develop apathy towards your audience and all those who come your way. You need to maintain your reputation and develop positive interactions with customers. In today's tech-dominated world, the need to have positive interactions with customers is more important than ever. It is important because of online reviews and feedback your business will receive on social media platforms. If you want to build solid relations, then you need good networking skills that can generate and ensure loyal customers. You need to exhibit a caring attitude and show some compassion towards your clients. You are running a business and your ability to succeed is directly proportional to your ability to communicate effectively with others.

Active Listening

In theory, active listening sounds simple. However, this is something that most people cannot seem to get the hang of. If you are just waiting for an opportunity to put in your two cents, then it is highly like that you aren't actually listening to what the other person is saying and are just interested in conveying your point. Two cents aren't worth much; just ask the economy the damage that inflation has done to the penny. These days, everyone seems to be eager to share their opinions, that it has all turned into noise. Did you know that there are more than 50 million tweets posted daily? The best way to get value for what you are saying is to value and respect what others have to say.

If you have managed to engage with your audience, then the things that you are saying seemingly become more interesting. Your audience can be anyone; it can be your colleague, your family members, or your friends as well. Learn the art of turning their interests into your own. In a conversation, you will need to be interested in what the other person is saying if you want them to listen to you. Once you have managed to establish that you genuinely care about what the other person is saying, the likelihood of them listening to you increases! This really isn't that complicated to understand.

Assertiveness

If you can stand up for yourself and for others in a calm and positive manner, then you are assertive. Being assertive means that you can do all this without being aggressive or passive. It is a tricky skill to perfect. There is a fine line between being assertive and being domineering. So, you need to tread carefully. Being assertive means that you can ask for what you want or solve a problem in a direct and respectful manner that conveys your point. It is easy to learn and is necessary for every entrepreneur.

You must never be too assertive, or it will make you seem arrogant or even unapproachable. It is important to practice this skill so that you can tread the fine line between being assertive and seeming domineering. It is important to practice it so that you don't cross the line. By being assertive you can express your vision, communicate your plan, and clearly define your objectives with the necessary confidence. Assertiveness is one skill that will come in quite handy when you have to deal with a conflict.

Communication

Effective communication is so much more than merely being able to talk to others. Being an effective communicator takes some practice and you need to work on your verbal as well as non-verbal skills. The ability to speak clearly and effectively will help you get your selling point across to others, and it will help others see what you can offer and the value they can gain. The better you can get your point across in a precise way, the more likely it is that the audience or your target customers will be receptive to your offer. To communicate effectively you must be able to stay calm, polite, focused, interested, and must also be able to match the mood of the situation. If you want to make the other person feel like you are interested and engaged in the conversation, then you need to speak thoughtfully and slowly. If you don't want your target audience to feel uncomfortable or confused, then you need to avoid talking fast and try to limit the usage of industry lingo. You need to consider your audience and the person you are talking to. You need to be able to adapt to their style to appeal to them.

Non-verbal communication is as important as verbal communication. Non-verbal communication is quite critical when you are meeting someone. You need to use positive non-verbal cues like open hand gestures and smiles. You must not only be mindful of your non-verbal communication, but you must also notice the non-verbal cues of the other person. Non-verbal communication includes facial expressions, hand gestures, voice, and posture.

Self-Management

It is important to manage yourself and your emotions especially to prevent a tough conversation from escalating. As an entrepreneur, you need to step up and accept the role of a leader. One of the pillars of leadership is self-management. While dealing with your target audience or your customers, there are times when things can escalate and take a turn for the worse. There is never a good time to show your true colors when you are dealing with customers. You need to have the necessary emotional intelligence to deal with your anger, frustration, and other negative emotions and replace them with desirable emotions like calmness and positivity. When you can control your emotions and yourself, that's when you can be truly composed. You must not let your emotions guide you and must always weigh your actions before you react.

You need to practice these interpersonal skills if you want to cultivate and develop good relations in your line of work. In fact, these skills will come in handy in your personal life as well. These interpersonal skills will help you hone your strengths and overcome any weaknesses you might have. Armed with these skills you can successfully mitigate and navigate any stressful situation.

Effective business networking takes place when individuals who trust one another become active advertisers of one another. If you want to develop your networking skills, then here are a couple of things that you must always keep in mind.

You need to understand that networking is all about being authentic. A relationship will prosper only when it is based on trust and authenticity. There are different business and entrepreneurial networking meetings that you can participate in to build your network. These meetings will help you connect with other groups and individuals who can help you achieve your goals. Not just that, these meetings also serve as a means to learn more about the entrepreneurial world and gauge your competition. You need to visit as many groups as you can so that you can meet someone who will spark your interest. Whenever you are trying to network with someone, the best way to do so is to ask open-ended questions. Avoid asking any questions that can be answered in a word or two. The best way to develop a relationship with someone is to talk to them. So, strike a conversation and make it as lively as possible. Others need to see you as a powerful resource. Only when they see you as a valuable resource will they want to associate themselves with you. It also increases your visibility. You must always have a clear understanding of what you do, your reasons for it, and the unique value you offer. If you have a precise answer to these questions, then it will set you apart from all your competitors. If you are given a referral, then don't waste any time taking the necessary action. You need to quickly act on a referral. After all, it is a referral and you need to respect and honor them if you want to grow in life. Also, make a point to call those who you meet.

Chapter Four: Building Your Eco-System

In this section, you will learn about the ideal platforms for affiliate marketing, things to keep in mind when you opt for social media marketing, and tips to create lead magnets.

Affiliate Websites

Amazon Associates

Amazon is one of the most popular websites these days. It is an online marketplace that connects buyers and sellers. You can pretty much buy anything under the sun on Amazon. In fact, you can order anything from candy to electronic gadgets. It offers great niche markets and, therefore, it is an ideal space to start an affiliate marketing venture.

Pros:
It offers up to 10% on any product sale that is directed from your link. You can generate affiliate revenue from all the purchases that the referred traffic makes even if it is not directly from the product you are linked to. It is a one-stop shop for a lot of people and offers a massive selection of diverse products.

Cons:
The affiliate cookies generated on Amazon last for only 24-hours. If the referred traffic comes and makes a purchase after 24-hours, you will not earn anything. There are limited options for payout like cheque, bank transfers, or Amazon gift cards.

ShareASale Affiliates

It has been in business for about 17 years and it is certainly updated with all the tech advancements. It is a marketplace for merchants and caters to everything that you can think of. Therefore, there will always be some product or other that you can promote as an affiliate.

Pros:

It offers different payout options like digital payments. There is a wide selection of products available. So, you have the option to pick a profitable product to work with.

Cons:

On the downside, it is not as straightforward as its competitors. It is not a major drawback, but you need a little technical knowledge to work with this platform.

eBay Partners

eBay is a user-based marketplace and you can use it to advertise and sell items on this platform. All that you need to do is find some listings that interest you and then you need to promote them using eBay's Partner Network to get paid for your work.

Pros:

There is no other marketplace on the Internet that offers the diversification that eBay does. You can pretty much sell any legal product that you can think of and no other platform can compete with eBay on the product diversification it offers. There are no technical or complex rules that you need to follow when you use eBay. You need to promote a product, and whenever someone buys using the link you promote, you earn revenue. It also offers a double commission for the first three months you are enlisted with this service.

Cons:

If a specific auction exceeds ten days, then you will not earn anything. There are three parties involved on this platform: you, eBay, and the affiliate. It means that the sales revenue will be split three ways. You will earn a percentage of what eBay will earn from the sale on its site.

Shopify Affiliate Program

One of the leading eCommerce platforms available is Shopify. If you have a niche audience, then this is the perfect platform to cater to their needs.

Pros:

You earn per referral that you make. During the first two months of the referral's subscription fee, you can earn up to 200% of the subscription fee you pay. It is a great platform to earn from referrals. In fact, you will earn per referral.

Cons:

Shopify is an ideal platform only if you are into a niche product. You need a specific audience to cater to and only then it will make sense to use Shopify.

Clickbank

This platform is quite similar to ShareASale. It is a diverse marketplace that is full of merchants from which you can pick something to promote. The merchant you decide to promote will depend on your target audience.

Pros:

It is quite likely that you will find some product or other to promote, given their vast product database.

Cons:

On the downside, they don't have any option for digital modes of payment. The only payment options they offer are cheque, direct deposit, or wire transfers. Regardless of the product you decide to promote, you cannot earn more than $150 per referral sale that is made.

Rakuten Marketing Affiliates

It is an online store that stocks everything from high-priced electronics to pet supplies. If you need something, it is quite likely that you can find it listed on Rakuten. The best part about using this platform is that they will pay you when you help them sell anything on their store.

Pros:

It is one of the most trusted online marketplaces. In fact, it has partnerships with well-established brands like NBA.

Cons:

You will need to individually apply to all the brands that you want to promote. It might take a little extra time, but then again, it does make sense to be prudent about the products you decide to promote. The knowledge base that it offers is difficult to navigate, but they do have a good affiliate support team in place.

Leadpages Partner Program

It is a powerful tool for online marketing. Every individual, regardless of their level of expertise, has the opportunity to create landing pages that help with conversions. The products they offer are unrivaled in their space. If you have a digital audience you want to cater to, then you must consider this platform.

Pros:

If you have the right audience, then it pretty much sells itself. The team at Leadpages does a good job with their products that you merely need to show those with websites that the tools exist to get sales. It is powerful and is certainly worth promoting. Also, they offer a commission of up to 30% on referral sales.

Cons:

On the downside, it might be too niche for a lot of affiliate marketers to work with. It sells well, but it will only sell to an audience who are trying to achieve something from their respective websites.

StudioPress Affiliate Website

It is a niche website, but it is certainly worthwhile if you have a good digital audience presence. This website helps create responsive, adaptable, and customizable WordPress hosting and themes that increase the function as well as accessibility of WordPress.

Pros:

It is another product that tends to sell itself. Most WordPress users need to just take one look at the tools this website offers and all that they can achieve with it. It does make your job significantly easier.

The payouts they offer are quite generous and you can get up to 35% per theme sale and a minimum of $75 per site sale that you make.

Cons:
The only problem with this platform is that it is quite a niche. It will benefit your audience only if they want to establish an online presence for themselves.

CJ Affiliate Publisher's Program

It is a platform that certainly knows what they are all about. They have been in the industry of affiliate marketing for over 19 years now. It will be quite difficult to find any fault with this program, given that they have products in every niche that you can think of.

Pros:
It is one of the largest networks of affiliates and it is difficult to rival them in size. If they have been in business for as long as they have been, then it does make them an expert.

Cons:
The process of application is quite difficult, and it is quite scrutinous.

Picking the Right Affiliate Program

Now that we've gone into the list of reputed affiliate networks it's important to know how to choose an affiliate program that's good for you. All affiliate programs are different and you need to thoroughly inspect each one before you decide to jump into a deal. This section will cover the various things that you need to keep in my mind when finding the program that's the right fit for you.

Terms and Conditions

If you have decided on which company is best for you and your customers, it's time to talk about terms. After all, that's what it's all about. The first thing to ask is how the program works. Are you paid purely for sales, or do you get a commission for leads? It is always better to argue for the latter as you will be tying up with someone who is considering you for your popularity. So, it is a good idea to optimally use this opportunity and argue in your favor. It can make a big difference when it comes down to dollars, both in the amount you can expect to earn, and how long you will have to wait to get paid.

How often do you get paid, and what is the minimum payout level? Many companies pay at the beginning or end of the month, or they may pay out twice a month – usually on the 15th and last day of the month. If you have a certain preference, then you can consider asking them to change the date of payout. Check that the minimum payment threshold is not set too high. Obviously, it's not cost effective to pay out every time somebody clears $10, but if you have to rack up $100 or more before you see the color of your commission, it can be very de-motivating, unless you have a high conversion rate.

Finally, you need to know the rate of commission – both the bottom line and the structure. Some businesses operate a two-tier system, where you get paid for everyone who clicks through to your affiliate, and then receive a further commission if they complete a purchase. Other businesses just pay for one or the other. Commission rates for affiliates vary considerably, from less than one percent for clicks to as much as 75% for some digital download products.

However, it's more realistic to work on a figure between 5% and 20%, and it's worth comparing similar companies to see if their commission rates and terms and conditions are similar.

Remember that money is important, but you will also have to consider several other factors that will help you judge whether the products and services offered comply with your standards. You cannot simply give anybody a nod and must lay down some ground rules for them. This might seem like the wrong thing to do but you need to maintain the standard of your blog and website as well. For this, you can send them a mail, listing the things that you will not be okay with on your blog or site, such as sexually explicit content, weapons, adult products, etc. There are companies who will be looking for people that are interested in letting out some space for such items. If they suspect that you have not explicitly mentioned these terms, they might start supplying you with links to such products. So, it is important for you to try to check everything that they send across, just to be cautious.

You must also discuss the rights and obligations and agree upon a termination clause. Remember, if you follow a path that is extremely professional, then it will be easy for you. You cannot take anything too lightly or casually, especially during the initial stages. Make sure you have everything signed and attested just to maintain an official record of your alliance and agreement. Once you are satisfied with everything and have made up your mind to go ahead with the deal then there must be nothing in the way to stop you.

Avoid Paid-for Programs

When you type 'Affiliate Marketing Programs' into Google, you will be inundated with hits. Some of these will be companies who ask you to pay to join their program. They will make use of fancy pamphlets that you can download and mention a well thought out payment plan. What's more, they will probably offer you a huge 'discount' to climb on board. The program's normal sign up cost is $99, but for today only, you will be admitted for the special price of just $20 – it may even be less than that. They will, in fact, make it look extremely attractive by canceling out the $99 with a big red cross and write $20 only next to it. All you have to do now is close the window and move away from such programs.

It goes without saying that there are a million suspicious websites out there, all of whom promise you something but do something else. Now, not saying that these people might cheat you, but even if they are to charge you a high amount of money it will be for their profit and they will not be bothered about you or your website. So don't trust these and only trust your instincts in doing the right thing.

As has already been noted, the affiliate business doesn't pay any commission to you until they make a sale, and remember this is a sale they wouldn't ace without your help. So why would they want you to pay for the privilege of widening their retail reach? It was mentioned before that nobody would be willing to part with their money just to promote someone else. That's like saying Microsoft wants to hire you but you need to pay the fees for it.

It can sometimes feel like the right choice to make, especially if the website you visited is promising you many things. I am sure you have also considered it many times just to get started with affiliate marketing at the earliest. You must be more patient when it comes to affiliate marketing, because otherwise, you might end up getting scammed.

But who in their right senses will use their credit card details or check into their online banking account to transfer money to a suspicious source? Not only is it dangerous for your account, but what if you end up the victim of identity theft?

So, as a rule of thumb, don't trust any website on affiliate marketing that promises you good business if you pay them some money first. That is not how it works and you will have to find a different way in order for you to establish a proper affiliate marketing set up.

Remember, if you stay too long on a website you will be tempted to check it out in detail. Instead, choose to exit as soon as possible and also clear your cookies.

Another thing that happens is that companies charge affiliates to join deals in high-ticket items. You may make a tasty profit from each conversion, but realistically are the people who will be visiting your site going to be interested in high-ticket stuff, even if it is linked to your niche? Even if you can answer 'yes' to that one, you're a beginner in the affiliate marketing game. Isn't it better to make your mistakes for free?

Check the Business

We've established that any affiliate you pair with must complement and add value to your site for your visitors, as well as return an income for you. We read on how it is possible for you to increase the number of customers that visit the affiliates page and how much more business both of you can establish together if you understand each other well.

But in order for this to happen, you must initiate the process of looking for the best affiliates to tie up with. So, make sure that you do some research and try and choose the best one. After all, you have the choice to nod or refuse a certain client depending on whether or not you like them.

One way to look for the good ones is by checking out what other blogs like you are hosting. You can randomly check the websites that other bloggers like you are hosting, especially the popular ones. Once you have a few, you can decide to contact them yourself and show them your blog or website. After you get a reply, you can skim through all the important ones.

Maybe you've looked at a few business websites and are wondering whom to approach. You can decide to shortlist 5 or 6 of them and go to the next step.

The first thing to do is check out the website for navigation. Is it easy to find the products your visitors will be interested in, and how easy is it to complete the purchase once the affiliate link takes the reader to the product?

This is important because you have to believe in the website yourself before you decide to host them for others. You will have to place yourself in the shoes of others just so that you have a chance to look at your blog from a third-party perspective. For this, you must understand how the affiliate website operates.

One way to check this is to place an order on the site yourself, so you can check out the purchase process on behalf of your visitors. Is the navigation process straightforward, from adding the item to your virtual basket? Is it possible for you to edit the items present in your cart? Can you increase or decrease the volume of the products easily? Does it have an option to add a coupon code? Is it possible to redeem any points? What about the payment process? Does the site support PayPal?

Many online purchasers are wary about using credit cards online and prefer the speed, simplicity, and security of paying via PayPal. And it's worth returning an item so that you can check out their standard of customer service. By placing affiliate links on your site, you are effectively endorsing the company and its products to your followers, so you need to know they will get good service.

Imagine what would happen if you start putting links to websites that are slightly tough to navigate or the buying process is complicated? People won't be interested in clicking on the links and the company might not garner as many hits as is necessary.

Once you've checked out that side of the business, and are completely satisfied with what you have, it's time to speak to someone about becoming an affiliate, so that any queries you have can be addressed before you commit yourself.

Make sure you have everything sorted out and jot down the questions in terms of importance and priority. Once sorted, start asking them one by one if it is a telephone chat, or you can also shoot them a mail with all your queries. Remember, it is never a bad idea to be well-informed about something. After all, you are hosting their website and it is best that they give answers to everything that you wish to know. It might take them some time to get back to you, and you can give them a couple of days to go through all your questions and answer them one by one.

If nobody is available to you, or they keep you waiting for several days for a reply, maybe you should move on. After all, if they can't make the effort to answer your queries before you become a partner, it isn't likely that they will do so once you've joined the program. So, don't keep waiting on someone that is not keen on replying to you, even if they say things like, "Sorry for the delay, we regret it."

Lead Magnets

Do you want to increase your list of email subscribers? One of the best ways in which you can do this is by offering a lead magnet. It simply means that you need to offer some valuable content in exchange for someone's email address. Hopefully, you are not trying to make people join your subscriber's list by saying, "Hello, subscribe to my newsletter." If you are doing this, then you are essentially saying, "Hello, I will be sending you a lot of emails." One thing that no one wants is a lot of emails. In this section, you will learn about the different methods that you can use to increase your email subscribers.

Resource List

People always love lists of tools and resources that they can use to gain something. You can create a list of simple items that you can deliver for a value and people will be more willing to subscribe. For instance, if you have a blog about fashion, then you can provide people with a list of the five best shopping websites or tips to dress well. Almost any sort of list will work, but you need to keep in mind a couple of simple rules when you decide to make a listicle. The content needs to be simple and it needs to be of some use to the reader. So, if you decide to use a resource list, then spend some time curating good listicles. If the listicle is interesting, then people will be more than willing to share their email address.

Quick-Start Guide

If you can teach people something that they can do quickly and without too much hassle, then it is a good way of obtaining their email address. If you have a photography blog, then you can offer them a quick-start guide about a specific camera or a way to use Photoshop quickly. Offering a quick-start guide is an easy way to pique the reader's curiosity and grow your email list.

Cheat Sheet

As the name suggests, a cheat sheet is typically a one- or two-page PDF file that contains tips that can help a person go through a specific process that would otherwise take them longer. A cheat sheet is like a quick-start guide, but it is more concise. For instance, you can offer a cheat sheet about the steps that a person can take to start a podcast or to start an online course.

A cheat sheet is like the Game Genie that people used to use while playing Nintendo. It is a device that you plug into the console and voila, you can walk through different levels much faster or start your game with 99 lives and such. So, like the Game Genie, the cheat sheet is a simple way in which you can gain some audience. You need to make sure that the cheat sheet contains practical steps that the reader can follow, and it must not be complicated or ambiguous to understand.

Video Answer

It is quite likely that your target audience will have a couple of pressing questions. So, you need to record a video answer for any such question. So, for someone who is new to your website, what is the first question that might pop into their mind? Answer this question on video, record it, and give them access to that video once they subscribe to your email list.

Checklist

Another great tool that you can use as a lead magnet is a checklist. For instance, if you teach social media marketing, then there are a couple of specific steps that a person needs to take to master social media marketing. You can provide them with a useful checklist in exchange for their email address. It can be anything that you want to provide a checklist for, as long as you are knowledgeable about it. Think about a process of your choice and then format a list with boxes that the reader can use to track their progress. You can provide them with this list in exchange for an email subscription. The idea is to provide something of value to your audience in exchange for their email address.

Email Scripts

If you want to teach people how they can communicate effectively via emails, then you can provide them with email scripts that they can repurpose and reuse for their communications. Writing emails is a cumbersome process and an email script can considerably simplify this process. It will help them save time and effort. So, make it easier for them by giving a simple point from which they can start.

Mini-Course

A mini-course is a short training program. It can be a short course or a portion of a longer course that you offer. Either way, it is a simple way in which you can offer value to your audience. When you give a mini-course for free, then you are essentially giving them a preview into all the value that they can gain. You can use this to upsell something else later on. For instance, you can offer a mini-course on how to use Adobe Premier to edit videos in return for email addresses. You can use this to promote yourself and also provide something valuable to the audience.

Instead of offering a mini-course that is present on a specific platform like Teachable, you can even offer them a mini-course that is based on emails. It is a great option to use email mini-courses because of the high value it offers. Not just that, it is quite easy to set up as well. Once someone subscribes to the email list, then they will receive a mini-course periodically.

Book Chapter

If you are marketing a book or are an affiliate marketer for a book, then you can offer the first chapter for free in exchange for the reader's email address. It is a really simple idea to generate a lead magnet. It is quite similar to providing a quick preview of the book. If the reader likes it, then it is quite likely that they will want to purchase the book. It helps create curiosity and interest in the mind of the reader. After all, sharing the email address is a small price to pay for a preview of the book.

Course Module

If you have an online course, then you can select a specific module from the course and provide it to your audience in exchange for their email address. It is a good way in which you can show people what the course is all about, and it increases the likelihood of spiking their interest in the course.

Quiz

You can offer a quiz along with its results to help people. You can offer a life score assessment quiz or something like that once the person signs up for your email list. It can be a quiz that you know will appeal to your target audience. You can offer a personality quiz, a Facebook Ads quiz or the like. It helps the audience and, at the same time, it helps you collect email addresses.

Template

If you are an entrepreneur who does a lot of teaching via platforms like YouTube, then you can offer a template to create something. For instance, if you want to teach about podcasting, then you can offer a free GarageBand file with a couple of audio elements that a person can use to start their own podcast. The objective of offering a template is to provide your audience with a head start. Well, who doesn't like a head start?

Transcript

If you do podcasts or online videos, then you can transcribe or the text file, convert it into a PDF file, and then offer it to your audience in exchange for their email address. Some people prefer reading instead of watching the video or listening to the podcast. Since it is a PDF file, the reader also has the option to print the file. You can provide them access to the transcript once they subscribe to your email list.

Bonus Audio

If you have a blog or website with a lot of articles, then you can take a couple of such articles and convert them into an audio file or MP3 file. This file can be downloaded, and the person can access it once they provide you with their email address. It is a great way in which you can repurpose existing content and will appeal to your audience if they are not interested in sitting down and reading something. Instead, they can listen to the audio file even when they are on the go.

Live Training

If you are into live teaching, then you can offer your audience free access to a specific webinar in exchange for their email address. So, you need to pick a date of a webinar you will conduct in the future and invite people to register for it. If you don't want to do this, you can also offer them access to a pre-recorded webinar. Once you create a live training video, then you can share this with others in return for their email address.

You can use any of these methods to grow your email list. Use an option that meets your goals and is in sync with what you offer.

Team for Affiliate Marketing

It is certainly no child's play to manage an affiliate program. You need to be a skilled negotiator, adept at reading and analyzing data, a good leader, and a heavy lifter who does all the work. All this might be too much for one person to manage. Therefore, it is a good idea to have a team in place that can help you with affiliate marketing. You might be good at one aspect of affiliate marketing but might need help with other aspects. There are five important aspects of affiliate marketing, and they are as follows:

Senior Strategist

The senior strategist is like the team leader who plans ahead and helps to keep the team focused. This person essentially creates a roadmap and understands all the aspects that one needs to undertake to become a successful affiliate marketer. The senior strategist plays the role of a mentor and guides the team towards success. The senior strategist always updates himself or herself about all the new developments that keep popping up in the field of affiliate marketing.

Affiliate Manager

The affiliate manager possesses good negotiation and people skills. The primary responsibility is to optimize the affiliates. This person is the "face" of the program. A good affiliate manager manages all relationships with customers, target audience, and other collaborators.

Data Analyst

To create a good affiliate marketing program, there is a lot of data that needs to be analyzed to optimize the program. This person is good with numbers and performs the role of a trend spotter. This person handles everything that has to do with crunching numbers and helps cut through all the clutter and discover any new opportunities. Apart from this, the data analyst also helps spot fraudulent or questionable activities.

Ad Operations

The ad operations and technology specialist is someone with a technical background. The primary job description of this person is to make sure that the link tracking is working properly, uploading creative elements and making sure that the backend is working efficiently.

Well, these are the different aspects that you need to consider if you want to become an affiliate marketer. There might be certain skills that you possess which make you good at a particular aspect of affiliate marketing. It is likely that you might not be good at all aspects and might need some help. You can always hire specialists in that particular area to help you with your work. Also, if you want to expand your operations or you want perfection, then it always makes sense to hire a team to help you with operations.

Whether You Need a Team or Not?

You probably want to take up affiliate marketing because you want to start your own business, or perhaps you want to leave the world of business and do something in your home. You might or might not be too keen to hire a team to help you with affiliate marketing. Are you not certain if you want a team or whether you can do it all on your own? Read on and you will be able to answer this question.

Someone probably mentioned that you need to build a team or that you are the bottleneck in your business, and as soon as these words were uttered, the Echo Chamber started to repeat it. The Echo Chamber occurs when someone shares a specific opinion and then everyone starts to repeat it as if it is a fact instead of an opinion. New affiliates or entrepreneurs often wonder if they need to build a team to be successful. If you are a new affiliate, then here are a couple of things that you need to be aware of before you decide if you need a team.

You need to understand all the aspects of this field, and only then will you be able to become a better teacher. If you are a better teacher, then you can curate a better team and teach your employees. If you create a good team then you can make money. If you try to build a team before you even know what you are doing, then what can you possibly team them? Here are some common questions that every new affiliate marketer has to answer before they jump into the game.

Do I need to build a "real" business? Well, the advantage that affiliate marketing provides is that you can choose your lifestyle. It is a good idea to start small and, once you gain traction, you can consider expanding.

Do I need a team, or can I do it on my own? You don't have to worry about what everyone else thinks you must do. You need to do what you think suits you. You don't have to rely on someone else's success strategy. What might have worked for one person might not work for you.

Am I the bottleneck to my business? Well, to be fair, if you are just starting your business, how can you be a bottleneck? You need to test one campaign and only then can you gauge your effectiveness. You need to remember that if you are flying solo, then you need to do all the work. You must be willing to put in the necessary hours and the work. You will also need to learn a lot along the way and you must be ready to learn. If you think you are a good manager and are better at delegation, then you can hire a team.

What if I don't possess the necessary technical knowledge? You don't have to worry about this as long as you are willing to learn. The Internet is your friend and you need to remember this. If you think that you don't possess the necessary design skills, then you can learn all about it on YouTube or even a simple Google search can help you. If you are not interested in doing this, then you can always hire someone who can do it for you.

Now that you know the necessary skills that you need to become a successful affiliate marketer and the answers to the questions you have, it is time to make a decision. Take some time and think about all that you read in this chapter. It is entirely up to you whether you want a team or not.

Social Media Marketing

Social media marketing begins with an extensive plan and is backed up by solid research on your audience. The next step is to engage that audience at the same time as publishing and sharing high-quality content. Promoting that content on the social media platforms you have opted to use is an important step, as is encouraging your followers to do the same.

Social Media Platforms to Use

There are few people who have not heard of the likes of Facebook and Twitter, but there are other social media platforms that, used in the right way, can be very effective in your marketing campaign. We are going to look at the top seven of those and how they can help your social media marketing campaign.

Facebook

Facebook is inarguably the most popular social media platform, with more than 1.2 billion active users. It provides advertising for businesses of all kinds, paid and free. It also offers the opportunity to set up business pages as a way of keeping your audience in touch with what's going on, to allow you to build up your list of subscribers, and to engage directly with your audience.

Facebook Ads is a PPC (pay-per-click) advertising system, which allows you to target specific ads at specific audiences, and, as well as all of that, your audience and followers can share your content and "like" your posts to increase the number of people you are reaching.

Twitter

Twitter is a microblogging and networking platform with more than 200 million accounts currently active. It is a very popular platform for businesses, celebrities, and entrepreneurs to provide updates on a regular basis.

Twitter users can post regular updates, known as "tweets," no more than 140 characters long, which also gives Twitter compatibility with the SMS system as well. You can create a business page and use it as a way of attracting followers and getting updates to your audience. You can also use the Promoted Tweets feature that gives you access to a platform for paid advertising, getting the message across to an even wider audience.

Google+

With 540 million active accounts, Google+ is the second biggest social media site in the entire world. Google+ is fully integrated with all of the other important services provided by Google, making it an excellent choice for any business or individual setting up a social media marketing campaign.

Google+ is a professional platform that is aimed at business users, allowing them to form direct relationships with their customers and investors with features like live video conferencing. Your profile on Google+ will be linked to your listing on Google Places, which allows your business to appear on maps and in local searches.

Google+ is fully integrated with Google Places, Google Authorship and, it goes without saying, the biggest search engine on the Internet today.

LinkedIn

With 277 million active users, LinkedIn is aimed solely at the business world, unlike other social media sites, which are aimed at both business and personal users. With LinkedIn, you can create a Company Page, giving you the opportunity to showcase your company or business and reach out to potential customers.

It is the number one go-to place for professional connections, especially those in B2B, or Business-to-Business marketing, and it allows you to find and hire employees, or search for business leads by searching through profiles of other like-minded professionals.

Pinterest

Far from being a website where people just pin photos, Pinterest is rather unique in terms of both social media sites and in social media marketing. It has 70 million active users, making it a relative teenager in terms of popularity, but that number is rising fast. Pinterest is ideal for both business users and individuals, especially those that rely on visual media. This will be businesses in the fashion or jewelry markets, photography, design, any business that needs a visual presence.

Pinterest offers business accounts with added features, such as the ability to analyze results and promote specific pins. Your business profile can also be easily linked in with your other social media platforms, including Twitter and Facebook.

Instagram

Instagram is another social media site that is aimed mainly at visual media, both photographic and video. It has over 150 million monthly active users and is the most popular of all the visual social media sites. It is perfect for businesses that err toward visual media, such as the fashion business, food, design, travel, and technology. Businesses can post photos and video of their products, use Instagram to host photo or video contests, and also integrate promotion codes.

You are only able to link your Instagram account to a business website but you can mention it in posts that you made on social media sites to generate more interest and traffic.

YouTube

YouTube is not strictly speaking a social media website but it is the most visited video sharing website and the third most visited website in the world. YouTube integrates a number of social features that make it a vital tool in your social media marketing campaign.

YouTube is a free platform that you can use to publish videos – maybe tutorials on how to use your product or service, reviews of products, and much more besides. It has its own program for paid advertising, which means your ads can show up on other people's videos.

Some of the important social features that are integrated with YouTube are the ability for people to comment on your video, share your content on Facebook, Twitter, Google+ and others and like or dislike your content, providing you with a rating on the site.

These seven social media networks revolve mainly around sharing your content, building up relationships, and generally giving you a solid online presence. This list is certainly not exhaustive; there are many more social media websites at your disposal as well.

How to Succeed with Social Media

The idea behind social media marketing is to always be there, to be able to directly engage with your audience. At the same time, this social media market is pretty much unorganized and with little control. Because of that, it is important to have a solid strategy if you are to succeed, a strategy that points you towards the right audience and gets you involved in the global reach of social media. If I haven't yet managed to convince you that social media offers a huge potential to your business, think about the following:

According to research done by Social Media Examiner, an online magazine, more than 86% of marketers asked said that social media was essential to them and their business. 49% of those use Facebook as their main platform.

Research carried out by WebDAM Solutions found that 43% of the marketers asked found some of their customers through LinkedIn and 52% found theirs on Facebook.

Research from Pew Research found that around 73% of all Internet users polled used social media in some format, with Facebook coming out as the most popular.

So, from that, you must be able to determine that social media is huge; it is the commonly used tool for businesses of all sizes and it is growing at a rapid pace. How can it help you? Let's look at some of the key areas that social media can help you in your business.

Social Media can:

Help you to tap into one of the biggest audiences in the world and generate global awareness of your products and/or services.

Help you to generate new leads and speed the process up by allowing you to create promotions and events.

Help to push traffic to your website and any other online portal that you have through the promotion of your content on social media sites.

Help you to build and maintain relationships directly with your customers and with potential customers so that you can promote your product or service in a better way and get to know your audience.

Help you to provide a good service and give your customers advice directly and then receive feedback from them to help you track how successful or not you are.

Help you to share your content and allow others to share it with their friends, family and followers, allowing them to do your advertising for you.

These are just some of the top reasons why you should be involved in social media marketing, but there are plenty more; it all depends on the type of business you are running. Social media platforms are an excellent medium for local businesses, especially those platforms that target the traditional high-street business. Look at platforms like FourSquare, Yelp, Google Places, and Bing Places. These will all help your business to appear in the local search results and en masse, whether they are mobile maps or online maps.

The best part about this is that all those platforms are completely free to use, and while you can go down the route of paying for social media marketing platforms, it isn't in your best interests to ignore the ones that are free.

Tips for Social Media Marketing Success

Social media is something of a confusing jungle and it is very easy to lose your way. Each individual platform has its own set of rules and formats and, if you want to succeed, you must learn the basics of each one first. There will be time to expand your knowledge later on as you get used to the ones you choose to use.

If you have decided that social media marketing is the way to go for your business, you will find these 25 tips invaluable.

Use only the platforms that are right for your business needs

Just because you opt to include social media in your business-marketing plan, it doesn't mean that you need to use every single platform available. For a start, it will take you too much time to learn each one and then implement a plan. Nobody, not even the most experienced of marketers, can handle more than a few of these accounts at any one time to go through each one carefully; look at what it has to offer and determine if it is the right one to market your business. The likes of Twitter and Facebook may have the largest number of subscribers but that doesn't mean that they have the right numbers of your target audience. You might find a better choice is one of the smaller platforms.

Evaluate Everything

There is only one way to determine if your efforts are working effectively and that is to evaluate all of the data. Some social media platforms have tools built in to help you do this and there are plenty of third-party options for analytic tools. Make use of these to look at what gets the most response in terms of the content you are sharing or promoting and, just as importantly, what isn't getting the level of response that you need. That way, you can figure what to drop and what to keep on doing.

Make Sure You Post at the Right Time

It isn't just what you are posting that has an effect of the numbers of people that see it, it is the amount that interact with it and share it. The timing of your posts is vital – most B2B businesses tend to stick to posting during normal working hours, but even then, some days will elicit a far better response than others. Do your homework – know when your target audience is likely to be online and schedule your posts to go live when they are there.

Build Your Connections

One of the most common mistakes that social media marketers make is to talk at their audience, rather than to them. Talk to your followers, engage with them, and interact with them. They want to know that you are human, not just some computer churning out automatic responses. Ask them to share their thoughts and make sure that you respond to their comments in good time. If they send you messages, communicate with them straight away; effectively ignoring potential customers will simply drive them away.

Go Visual

People are put off by large blocks of text but they stop and take notice of images. Photos, videos, and infographics have information in them that people tend to take in easier. Make sure your visual content is strong, appealing, and relevant to your business.

Make Each of Your Chosen Platforms Unique

There are plenty of tools that allow you to share content across several platforms but, while this might work for information that is highly important, doing it for every piece will simply make all of your platforms identical. People that follow you on one platform are likely to follow you on all of them and they do not want to see identical content – that will ensure they only follow you on only one. Make each of your accounts unique, and that will draw more people in and gain you more followers and more potential customers.

Make it Worthwhile for People to Follow You

When someone follows you on a social media account, they want to feel some kind of appreciation for that. Offer up rewards for subscribing or following you – maybe a small discount on a product or entries into a prize draw. People need an incentive to join you and it will keep them engaged and interested if they get something out of it.

Be a "Personable" Person

While social media may be a more relaxed manner of marketing your business, you still need to maintain an air of professionalism. Yes, do give out some personal details that will give your business that human face, like a birthday or a bit of banter here and there, but never start giving out your personal views on things on your business page. If you start getting hot under the collar about politics or talking down the latest celebrity gaffe, you can very easily start to turn your followers away from you.

Have a Social Media Manager

It might be seen as a non-job but it is amazing the results that a proper social media manager can obtain. Not everyone is proficient at social media and, if you are not, it is better to have someone at the helm who can converse with others, engage easily, like posts, and share content easily. That way, you can get on with running your business and reap the rewards of a successful marketing campaign.

If it isn't Working, Ditch it

Not everything is going to work; it doesn't matter how much analysis you do, how many new team members you recruit, there will be that one platform that simply isn't right for your business. If nothing is working, and you are not gaining any results from it, ditch it and walk away. There are better things for your time and energy to be used on.

Build up Relationships with Businesses

If there are businesses that are in the same sector as you or the same industry, friend them and follow them, but only if they are not direct competition. You may be able to refer customers to each other, share followers, and pick up tips. It might just surprise you how much good can come of this so give it a go but don't friend or follow everyone indiscriminately – be choosy.

Face the Trolls

The more successful you become, the more attention your social media accounts will draw. And that means the inevitable abuse from some people. If you find that you have haters on your pages, be professional in your dealings with them. Choose carefully how to respond – sometime it must be a polite response, other times, it works better to ignore them and, in some cases, you will need to block them. Do not block someone just because they don't like your company; that is not good business sense and it doesn't send out a good message.

Leave Your Work at Work

Everyone works too hard and, when you are just starting out in business, it is tempting to be there 24/7 to keep an eye on things. Mobile technology has made it possible to be "at work" all the time, but unless you really are a glutton for punishment and you still want to be responding to Facebook or Twitter comments in the middle of the night, don't download the apps onto your mobile. When the working day is over, walk away and leave it for the next day.

Don't Keep on Selling

I know this is why you are in business but when it comes to social media, it is a huge sin. People who follow you do not want to be bombarded with sales pitches every five minutes. They are not there to do you a favor, they want to enjoy themselves and learn. They want to build up relationships and look for entertainment. When they want to buy, they will come and find you, be it on social media, your website, or some other portal.

Make Sure Your Business Profile is Fully Completed

On your profile, you are given plenty of space to give your followers information about you. Leaving parts of it blank will not endear you to any of your followers; they want to know all about you, they want to know what makes you worth following and supporting. Blank spaces say that you are not interesting and nobody will take the time to follow someone who can't even complete their profile.

Make Social Media Part of Your Plan

Think of this as just another area of your business; it needs to be goal oriented and you need objectives written into your business plan. This makes it easier to measure just how worthwhile social media is to your overall plan

Make Your Followers Want to See Your Updates

The ultimate goal of any marketing plan is to make people want to read your content. You want these people to be hanging on every word you write, to be eager to see the next installment. You want them to be checking constantly to see if you posted anything, and the only way to do this is with high quality, valuable, relevant content.

Make it Easy to Share Your Content

While the age of technology has made it possible for us to do as little as possible, if you want your content shared, you are going to need to do some work. You must package your content in a way that makes it easy to be shared and give people the buttons that they need to send on the content to a friend or to another of their own social media pages. Make it so easy for them to do it that it will be harder for them not to do it.

If You Share something, Comment on it

Don't just click on the button that lets you share something or retweet it; add a comment to it to tell people why you think the content is worth sharing. This helps you to build up your own expertise and a reputation for being that expert. That adds a lot of value to whatever you are sharing.

Check Your Grammar and Spelling

This is important. You are a professional businessperson and the worst thing you can do is publish content that is badly written and full of spelling mistakes. Check your work, double check it and then check it again to make sure it is professionally written before you publish

Learn the Difference between a Reply and a Mention

When you begin a tweet with a username, the only people that will see the tweet are you, the person mentioned, and anyone who follows your or that user. Placing the username somewhere in the middle of the text makes it visible to those who follow you or that user. If you want to talk about a specific person and want everyone to see it, you just put the name in the center of the post, not at the beginning. However, if it makes more sense that the post has the username at the beginning, add a full stop in front and it will be classed as a Mention, not a Reply

Never Post on the Hour

Most meetings and tasks are scheduled to start at the top of the hour. So, when the clock strikes, people are moving on to the next item on their list, not looking at their social media accounts. If a task or meeting finishes early or overruns a bit, that gives a small window to check those accounts. Therefore, it makes sense to post your content just before or just after the hour, not on it. This way, more people will see what you are posting.

Interact with those Who Share Your Content

If someone shares a link to your latest content or retweets a message, take the time to thank them. These are the people you want to keep on your side, the people that are carrying out a lot of free advertising for you. Build up a good relationship with them and make them want to keep on sharing your content.

Learn the Platform Guidelines

Familiarize yourself with the guidelines that each platform has, make sure you know what is and isn't acceptable in terms of behavior and content. Common sense must dictate what kinds of content; you need to check up on the terms and conditions for the platform before you post on it. Some, in particular, Facebook, are constantly changing their guidelines on things like running competitions, and breaching those can result in a penalty, suspension, or complete expulsion from the platform, and that is not what you want for your business.

Make Sure Your Profile includes Your Location

People need to know where your business is based, even if your service or product is Internet based so it can be used or go anywhere. If they know where you are, they can find you and check in, particularly on Facebook. This is more important if you have a physical store that people can visit – not adding your location can lose you a lot of potential customers.

YouTube Videos

YouTube has grown into an influential social media platform. What started out as a fun medium of introducing the world to three-dimensional interaction has now turned into a powerful tool for marketing. Just like in every other social media channel, the secret to success is getting a following or audience to broadcast your videos to. The more views you get, the more popular your videos will be and the greater success you will have in ranking highly in the search results. Here are some tips to get you started when creating and promoting your YouTube channel.

Setting It Up

When creating your YouTube channel, ensure that you use your company's name and any relevant branding resources to make sure that your channel is easily identifiable to your target audience. Also, ensure that you have a clear, catchy and straightforward company description. Look for ways of linking your YouTube channel to your other social media pages to provide cross-promotion. You can also do cross-promotion by linking your channel to other pages that you are affiliated with. When you start, the next step is to promote your channel to ensure that you get the most views to your videos. Here are some tips to get more views:

Videos

Videos subtly attract people to click on them when they show up in the search results. In this case, you must strive to shoot and upload all your videos in HD format. As such, you must ensure that your videos are shot in an environment with perfect lighting. You don't have to do hours of video to pass your message across. More people are likely to watch short videos than extremely long ones, so keep that in mind when creating videos.

A Good Thumbnail

To be honest, most of us only click on YouTube videos that already seem to be descriptive of what we are looking for. We mostly judge this by looking at the thumbnail. Therefore, ensure that you have one that is highly captivating to maximize clicks to your channel.

Use Trends

Although you shouldn't be misleading in your titles, using hot titles will increase your chances of attracting an audience through organic search. This works similarly with the thumbnail. A catchy thumbnail can enhance the number of views on your videos to a large extent.

Annotations

You can interlink YouTube videos through annotations (these can appear at the top left and at the top right corner of each video whereby the ones at the bottom link to the previous video while the ones at the top link to the next video). You can use annotations to develop a menu screen at the end of each video whereby the viewer is presented with other videos that he or she can choose from. With this option, it will be a lot easier for people to navigate between all your videos, which in turn results in more views. Additionally, you can use annotations to point users to a playlist or the page that prompts the viewers to subscribe to your channel.

Promote On Other Channels

Share your YouTube videos on other social media sites like Twitter and Facebook. Whenever you upload a video, share it to your networks and ask your friends to share it or like it as well. Ensure that each video has a clear call to action asking viewers to subscribe or share the videos. You can opt to use this in the middle or at the end of the video.

Captions

If you don't want to lock out people who have hearing problems, you can use captions in your YouTube videos (captions are simply YouTube's subtitles). These captions also come in handy for those who want to watch videos without turning on their volume. Additionally, the content is also searchable on YouTube's search, which in turn means you will find it easier to rank. To add captions, click edit a video then choose the captions tab.

Miscellaneous

Ensure that you have a consistent pattern of uploading new videos to your YouTube channel. This predictability is very critical if you want to have a dedicated following. Ensure that you engage your followers always by responding to comments, suggestions, and other forms of feedback from your audience. Your responses must be prompt. Partner with bloggers within your niche. These will probably be willing to share high quality and informative videos on their blogs. With this option, you will generate more leads, more views, and more subscribers. You will also have a valuable backlink to your video. Having your video embedded in a page with a high page rank increases your chances of ranking highly on YouTube. You might need to give them an incentive to promote your video on their blog.

Chapter Five: Walking the Talk!

Dress to Kill, Impress to Kill & Nail Deals!

As an entrepreneur, you need to learn to dress to impress. The essential rule for dressing that you need to keep in mind is that you need to adopt a style that is elegant, simple, and showcases your personality. When you are dressed well, it does improve your confidence.

It is important to make a good first impression especially when you are dealing with customers, your associates, or anyone else from the industry. If you need to make a presentation, then you need to be dressed for the occasion. There are different things that will determine the impression you manage to make. Your level of success depends on your verbal as well as non-verbal cues. Non-verbal cues include the way you dress and accessorize, the firmness of your handshake, your posture, and the manner in which you conduct yourself. The way you dress needs to convey your professionalism. In this section, you will learn about certain things that you need to keep in mind to dress to impress.

General Tips

You need to wear clothing that is professional and conservative. Choose those items of clothing that have received positive feedback from people who are knowledgeable about the industry. Make sure that every item of clothing that you wear is clean, pressed, and well-fitting. Always opt for conservative footwear. Choose accessories that will compliment your clothing and not act as a distraction. If you have any facial or body piercings, then perhaps you can remove them. Cover any visibly distracting tattoos. The fragrance you use must be subtle and must not be overpowering. You must always dress comfortably. If you wear something uncomfortable, then you will feel uncomfortable. Dressing comfortably doesn't mean that you dress like a slob. Dressing comfortably doesn't mean that you wear your sweatpants all day long. Regardless of what you wear, make sure that they fit you well and aren't a size too big or too small. Always opt for dark clothing since it looks more professional.

Tips for Women

Acceptable clothing for women includes a suit or a conservative well-tailored dress. You can opt for a skirt or a pair of slacks according to your level of comfort. If you decide to wear a dress or a skirt, then opt for something that is knee-length. Anything that is slightly shorter or longer will be acceptable. You must avoid blouses or sweaters that are form-fitting, have plunging necklines, are transparent, or have any other distracting details on them. Ideally, opt for clothing that covers your arms at least up to your biceps. If you decide to wear pantyhose, then make sure that it is plain and not patterned. The color must flatter and compliment your skin tone. Always opt for a neutral color and make sure that it is coordinated with your clothes. The perfume that you use must not be overwhelming and needs to be subtle. Don't paint your nails a dark or distracting color like red and opt for clear polish or something equally subdued. Apply minimal makeup, or you can always go for natural-looking makeup. Avoid loud colors. You can either carry a briefcase or a handbag, but not both. You can wear low-heeled pumps or flat shoes. Make sure that your footwear is clean and polished. You can accessorize your outfit, as long as you keep it minimal. You can wear small earrings, a sensible watch, and maybe a ring. Don't over-accessorize

Tips for Men

You need to wear a matching suit in a dark neutral color like navy blue, black, or gray. Alternatively, you can pair a dark jacket with light-colored dress slacks. You can opt for patterned (preferably pinstripes and nothing else) or solid clothing. Choose a white or light-blue colored dress shirt that contrasts with the jacket you wear. You need to ensure that your arms are fully covered. Exposing your arms or rolling up your sleeves makes the outfit informal and more casual. If you decide to wear a tie, then opt for a silk tie or something similar. The tie must be well coordinated with your jacket and your slacks, but it must be in contrast with your dress shirt. A half-Windsor knot is perfect for a professional setting. The socks you wear need to be at least calf-length and avoid ankle-length socks at all cost. Do not wear slip-ons and wear dress shoes, the lace-up kind. The color of your footwear must be dark and must blend well with your pants. Always opt for a leather belt that matches your shoes. Your hair needs to be cut short and you must not have any facial hair. Minimize the accessories you wear and limit it to one ring per hand. You can wear a sensible dress watch. You can wear a full-length coat over your suit, but you cannot wear any casual coats. Also, the cologne that you use needs to be subdued and not strong.

Presentation Skills- 5-10 Minutes Deal

Whether you want to raise some capital for your business or you just want to develop a better business strategy, you will need a good elevator pitch to achieve your goals. An elevator pitch is a speech that lasts less than a minute. This pitch is a summary that provides a bird's eye view of your business and the details of how you plan on being successful. In this chapter, you will learn about building a perfect elevator speech.

Defining the Problem

The first step for creating a winning elevator pitch is to identify a problem that's worth solving. If the product or service that you are offering doesn't solve a problem that your potential customers face, then it isn't viable. Now, the problem doesn't have to be anything massive or something that will change the world. Well, it's certainly great if you are tackling something like that, but for most businesses, this isn't the case. Problems can be simple and there's nothing wrong with that. As long as you can solve a problem that the customers are facing, you can have a viable business. Here are a couple of problem statements that you can make use of: "There are no good Oriental restaurants in Eugene, Oregon." "The process of analyzing results from MRI can be expensive and time-consuming." And so on. Describe your customer's problem in the simplest of terms, in one sentence.

Describe the Solution Offered

A lot of entrepreneurs tend to start their pitch by describing the solution they offer. They tend to skip the previous step. Avoid doing so and always state the problem before offering a solution to it. Explain the solution that you are offering in a clear and a concise manner without unnecessarily stretching it. Try to explain the solution in simple terms.

Your Target Market

Once you have defined the problem and have come up with a solution for the same, the next step will be to identify your potential customers. In this part of the pitch, you will have to define the audience you are catering to. Try to divide your target market into small segments and it gets easier to target them. It is quite tempting to let your target be as big as possible, but that doesn't help in making a credible elevator pitch. For instance, if you have a shoe company, your target audience cannot be "everyone with feet." Perhaps you are catering to a group of people like athletes. Once you have identified your target audience, you must divide them into smaller segments. For instance, athletes can be divided into walkers, hikers, runners, and so on.

Describing Your Competition

There is an alternative available for every problem. So, in this section of the speech, you will need to think about all the advantages that your solution has to offer compared to your competitors. Tell your audience why they must choose you and not the other candidates.

Your Team

A great idea is essential, but without a great team, that idea will just be an idea. In this part of your elevator pitch, describe why you and your business partners or team members are best suited for executing your goal. Include information that conveys that your team has precisely all the necessary skills. A vision needs to be executed by the perfect team and pitch your team too. If you must pitch yourself, then talk about your expertise and how it will be helpful in solving the problem you described earlier.

Financial Summary

The financial summary doesn't mean showing or presenting an elaborate five-year plan. It is important that you understand your business model well. Business model might sound slightly complicated; however, it is quite simple. You must simply know who is paying your bills and the kind of expenses you are bound to incur. A likely sales and budget forecast or estimate is what you need.

Showing Traction with Milestones

The final part of your elevator pitch is conveying your business milestones. Provide your audience with information about any upcoming goals and by when you plan to accomplish the goals you have established. Talking about your goals helps your pitch seem realistic. It also shows how well you have thought about your business or idea and what the potential customers can expect from you.

Write down all the different parts of the pitch and then put those different parts together. Make sure that they are in harmony.

How To Write Each Part

It will take a while to perfect your pitch. You will probably have to come up with multiple versions before you find one that fits the bill and is compelling without sounding robotic. Here are a couple of steps that will help you in writing the different parts of the elevator pitch.

Identifying Your Goal

The first step will be to identify the goal of your pitch. For instance, are you trying to convey information about your organization to your potential clients? Do you have a brilliant idea for developing a product or service? Or do you want to simply explain about yourself? Write down your goal or goals.

Explain What You Do

Once you have described what your organization is all about, focus on the problems that you can solve and how you can help others. If you can, add in a statistic or some information that shows the value addition that you can do. Ask yourself this simple question: "What do you want the listener to remember or take away from the speech?" Remember that your speech must be exciting. If you aren't excited about what you are saying, it is highly unlikely that your audience will be. Emotions are contagious, so remember to maintain your enthusiasm.

Communicating Your USP

Once you have figured out how to explain what you do, the next step is to write down your USP or your Unique Selling Proposition. This helps in identifying what makes you, your product or service, or your organization different from others. Think about the novelty that you have to offer.

Engaging with a Question

Once you have identified your USP, you will need to be able to engage your audience. You can do so by preparing an open-ended question that will get them involved in the conversation. Make sure that you have an answer to the questions that your listeners might have. Also, the question you come up with shouldn't force the listener to think too much. Since doing so will divert their minds and they won't listen to your pitch. Your question must make them ponder, but not too much.

Putting it all Together

Once you have completed all the different sections of your pitch, the final step is to put them all together. Then, read it out loud and time yourself. Make sure that you are sticking to the 30-second time limit. If you feel like it needs to be tweaked, then do so.

Once you have done all this, the next step is to keep practicing your pitch until you perfect it.

Practice

Like with anything else in life, practice makes you perfect. Remember, the way in which you deliver your speech is as important as what your speech is about. If you don't practice, then it is very likely that you will talk too fast, sound unnatural, or even forget something important that you had to convey. Make it a point to keep practicing your speech regularly. The more you practice, the more natural your speech will start to sound. Your pitch must flow naturally, it must be an extension of the conversation, and shouldn't sound like an aggressive sales or marketing pitch.

You must be aware of your body language while talking because it conveys as much information to your audience as the words you say. So, practice in front of a mirror or you can practice it in front of your family members, friends, or colleagues until it feels natural to you. Once you get used to delivering your speech, you can vary it slightly; the idea is to not sound like a robot, it shouldn't seem well rehearsed even if it is. There is a difference between customizing your elevator pitch and practicing it. Always have a set of points that you have to address while delivering your pitch, and practice different ways in which you can improvise certain points to suit the needs of the audience you are addressing. People will not be interested in listening to your pitch if you don't sound comfortable or confident while delivering it. Therefore, you must be well aware of the content you are using and being confident doesn't mean using all sorts of technical jargon. Use non-technical and informal language for your pitch, as the usage of difficult terminology can be off-putting and shows that you aren't able to simplify what you do. Apart from this, it can bore and confuse your audience. Practicing will make sure that you are able to sound natural without trying too hard.

Practice, practice, and practice a little more. If you want your audience to listen to what you are saying, then you will need to make sure that your pitch flows naturally and you don't stammer while talking. Sounding nervous or mechanical will simply detract the attention of the listener from the content you want to convey. So, practice your speech out loud and often until it comes out smoothly. Keep rehearsing. You have plenty of time to get it right and time is your ally. Write your pitch down, edit it, practice it on friends or others, and make necessary changes according to the feedback you receive. Practice it in front of the mirror before heading off to work and recite it once before you go to sleep. By the time you have to deliver your pitch, it will come to you naturally. Your brain will run on autopilot and you will be able to deliver it with ease.

Additional Tips

Your pitch needs to be short, precise, and easy to understand. Ideally, it must not exceed 5-7 minutes.

It needs to be persuasive: Even though it's brief, your pitch must be persuasive and it must spark an interest in the listener about your idea, business, or yourself.

Sharing your skills: It must quickly explain who you are, the qualifications you have, and the skills you possess. Focus on how your skill set will help in adding value to their lives or any situation. This is your chance to promote yourself. However, try not to sound boastful.

Practice is essential: Keep practicing your elevator pitch until you have perfected the speed and the "pitch" must come naturally to you, without sounding mechanical.

Always be flexible: Always appear open-minded and flexible. This is an opportunity to make a good impression with a prospective employer or client.

Always mention your goals: You don't have to go into specifications or technicalities. It must mention what you are looking for (your goals). It can be something like: "A role in human resource management," or perhaps, "An opportunity for applying my marketing skills to a new market," and so on.

Know your audience and speak to them: Using technical jargon does convey your knowledge of the industry. If you use a lot of technical terms during a pitch, it can backfire. Understand the audience around you and speak accordingly.

Always have a business card handy: If you have a business card, then offer this after your pitch. This will show your enthusiasm and preparedness as well.

Building Business Relationships

An important aspect of the business that a lot of people seem to neglect is building business relationships. It not only takes time but also energy to build and develop good and lasting business relationships. Business relationships are critical and a necessary part of success, but not a lot of people seem to know what needs to be done.

Note: If you want to create a business relationship that will last, then you need to understand that they don't just happen. You will need to cultivate them via dedicated and consistent efforts. You must be prepared to dedicate the necessary time and effort to develop them.

Your business network must consist of qualified and a selective group of individuals, whom you can count on, access and rely on for direction, insight, as well as support. You need to strike a balance between being a giver and a taker. You cannot just keep giving or taking, there needs to be a symbiotic relationship between the two. A lot of people don't ask for help when they are in desperate need of it, and if you make this mistake, it can be fatal to your dream of being an entrepreneur. In this section, you will learn about the different ways in which you can develop and strengthen business relationships in today's world.

Be Authentic

You need to be authentic. It is a simple concept. You need to not only be true to yourself, but also need to accept others as they are. It is easy to create a façade, especially online, but that is not a way in which you can develop a lasting relationship. If you create a false persona, the relationship you cultivate through it will have a short shelf life. You need to find people and other businesses with whom you feel a connection. There needs to be ease of communication with things you share. If you want to accelerate a relationship, then there needs to be authenticity in personality, beliefs, and opinions.

Shared Values and Goals

Knowingly or unknowingly, we all tend to look for people with similar goals and values. You need to see if they are honest, kind, helpful, resourceful, and knowledgeable. Not just that, you need to respect them as well. A lot of people merely present themselves in a specific manner to gain something from others once they have their trust. You might not always share the same opinions, but it is important to find someone with similar interests.

Mutual Respect

It takes time to develop mutual respect unless someone is referred to you by a third-party you trust. You need to prove yourself over time through various activities and experiences. It also takes time for you to respect someone. You can join an online community, a business group or a chamber if you want to develop business relationships. You need to be selective and patient when you decide to develop a business relationship with someone. Never rush into anything and watch people in action before you take the next step. If you want a relationship to grow and sustain itself, then there is a need for mutual respect.

Vulnerability

We are all human beings, and everyone has some vulnerability or other. At times, to develop a good relationship with someone, there is a need to share and support one another through a particularly challenging or difficult time. Showing your vulnerability at times makes you strong and it is necessary to maintain authenticity in the relationship. A word of caution: You need to share your vulnerabilities with a few select individuals and not everyone. Use your good judgment when it comes to this aspect of a business relationship.

Loyalty

You need to let others know that you have their back. It is a simple way in which you can show your loyalty to them. Gossip and unnecessary conversation can kill any relationship. It might be tricky to avoid such situations, but there is a way out. You can always politely ask the other person to reconsider their opinions about others or you can avoid interaction with such people.

Meaningful Connection

You need to make meaningful connections when you decide to network with others. In fact, the biggest compliment that you can get from others is a referral. You need to be thoughtful, have the right motives, and you need to connect with people for the right reasons. It is not necessary that every referral you get will work favorably for you. It does take two people to make it happen and you must not be doing all the work.

Personal

If you want to genuinely get to know people, you can meet them in person for coffee and talk to them. You must be open to sharing your experiences, ideas, opinions, and beliefs if you want to develop a lasting business relationship with someone.

Expectations

You need to let go of any expectations you have about any relationship you want to form. Nothing kills a relationship like expectations do. You need to keep an open mind and you must never assume anything. Accept others the way they are and not as something you want them to be. If you have any preconceived notion of how people are, then you will set yourself up for disappointment. Before you decide to ask someone for something, you need to offer something.

Sub-Affiliates

The term tier-two affiliate might be new to you, especially if you are new to the field of affiliate marketing. A tier-two affiliate is an intriguing feature of a specific affiliate program in which affiliates can sign up additional affiliates below them. So, whenever a sub-affiliate or a tier-two affiliate earns a commission, then the primary affiliate will receive a commission too.

In this two-tier system, the first tier of the commission that the primary affiliate receives is like that of any regular affiliate program. The only difference is that it has an additional tier or sub-affiliates, whereby the marketer earns a commission once the traffic that the sub-tiers referred to the program makes a sale. Theoretically speaking, an affiliate program can have multiple tiers, however, there are certain practical limitations that are inherent to this system. As the tiers increase, the affiliate program will draw out more webmasters whose sole aim is to gain profit from all the effort and work that others make.

The two-tier affiliate program is also known as multi-level marketing. When you decide to sign up for a specific affiliate program, then you are known as the first-tier affiliate marketer and the person that you recruit or encourage to sign up is the second-tier affiliate. If there are any additional tiers, then the system will be known as multi-tier marketing or multi-level marketing. This method of marketing isn't as successful today as it was a couple of years ago. It is because in today's world, affiliates have the option to freely select from multiple affiliate programs, and they have the opportunity to switch from one program to something else.

If you think that you can fully rely on the second-tier affiliate to do your work for you, then you are sadly mistaken. So, if you want to use a two-tier affiliate program and benefit from it, then you need to motivate the sub-affiliates to sign-up below you. You need to make sure that you select the affiliate vendor carefully. You must always opt for those merchants who generate a steady stream of high-quality products, give good commissions, offer the feature of real-time tracking, provide you with the correct numbers, and offer support. You can also sign-up with a vendor or a merchant who has a steady and high rate of visitors-to-sales conversion.

It is also important that you engage yourself with a platform that has a user-friendly website that you can access easily from anywhere and monitor your progress.

It will merely be a waste of your time and effort, or worse, it can damage your integrity as an affiliate marketer if you promote a poor affiliate program. Or at least that will the presumption it creates in the customer's mind and they will presume that the product or service you are promoting is dreadful too. Therefore, you need to always stick to good affiliate programs.

There are two significant advantages that a sub-affiliate provides. The first one is that the profit you earn will increase due to an increase in sales from the customers from the second-tier referrals. The second advantage is that you will have access to a wider customer base. So, it is up to you to consider whether you want a sub-affiliate or not.

Chapter Six: Your Product

How to Select a Product/Service?

Now that you want to become an affiliate marketer, the next step is to decide on the products that you want to promote. The product or service you decide to promote will decide your success as an affiliate marketer. When you try to select a specific product, here are a couple of questions that you need to ask yourself:

The product that you are leaning towards, does it have a professional appearance, does it have good product reviews and a sales page? What is the ideal market to sell this specific product to? Does this product belong to a niche that you are comfortable with? In this section, you will learn the different steps that you can follow to select an ideal product or service to promote as an affiliate marketer.

Make a List

The first thing that you need to do before you select a product to promote as an affiliate is to make a list of all those products that interest you. According to your chosen niche, you might come up with a long list of products that you find interesting. The next step is to narrow down the list you made by removing all those products that will not help you earn a decent commission. How can you do this? You need to go through different affiliate programs for the products that you like. Look at the commission you will earn for each of those products. If you think that the commission you will receive on a product is quite low, then you need to immediately eliminate it from your list. Always select those products that will help you earn at least $30 per sale made.

Market Niche

The next factor that you need to consider before you select a product to be an affiliate is to find the market niche for that specific product. The marketplace can be ideally divided into 23 primary categories. So, you need to go through all the categories available and select a product that you are comfortable with promoting. Whenever you select a product to be an affiliate marketer for, you need to choose to sort results by its market gravity. The gravity of a product is directly proportional to its sales. So, any product with a higher gravity will experience a higher rate of sales. The ideal market gravity of a product needs to be 20 or less. It might be tempting to select a product with a market gravity of more than 1oo. If a product has such high market gravity, it also means that the competition you will face will be quite tough. As a newbie, it is a good idea to avoid such products. If you do decide to opt for a product that has strong competition, then make sure that you have brilliant strategies to promote and market that product. An exceptionally good marketing strategy is the only thing that will help you succeed while facing stiff competition.

Market

The next factor that you need to consider before you select a product as an affiliate is a need for that specific product. You have the opportunity to earn a big commission from affiliate sales if the product you opt for will help solve a need or a desperate problem that customers have. There needs to be a healthy demand for the product on the market. If you do find a product that meets this criterion, then you can freeze that option. If you have a product that you think is a good fit for affiliate marketing, then you can select it. For instance, it is not a smart move to promote products related to ice skating when you know that winter is almost at an end. On the other hand, if you know that Christmas is nearing, then you can count on a lot of families cooking during the holidays, so you can select a product related to food.

Start Affiliate Marketing

The various steps and processes that are part of an affiliate program are given below:

As an affiliate, you first sign up with the advertiser either through an affiliate network or directly. After the contract is signed, you will get a special affiliate URL or link containing the affiliate's username/ID.

You then use this link for display on your website. Sometimes, the advertiser will send some creative content or banners to you that need to appear on your website. These details usually form part of the agreement.

When a visitor to your website clicks on the advertiser's link, a cookie from the advertiser is dropped onto the visitor's computer.

The customer then makes a purchase or does a required transaction on the advertiser's link.

When the visitor completes the transaction, the advertiser will check the cookie on the computer and find your affiliate ID and give you credit for the transaction.

The advertiser then updates all relevant reports that reflect visitor traffic as well as sales that your affiliate link has generated.

Commission payments are made on a regular basis, normally monthly, based on the sales and/or leads generated. These are clearly spelled out in the agreement contract signed by the advertiser and publisher.

Find Your Niche

The first and foremost thing to do is to find your niche. Before you get into blogging or starting your YouTube channel, you must first find the niche market where you can establish yourself. This will help you find your target customers. Before you get started with finding your niche here are some questions to ask.

What is it that interests me most?

How lucrative is the niche?

How much time will I put in?

How long will my business be profitable?

Are there affiliates available?

Research

The next step of the process is conducting your research. Once you decide on the niche, you have to find the programs and products that best suit your niche. You might have already started with it while deciding on your niche and now it is time to do a little more research on it.

You have to spend some amount of time going through the programs and what they offer to you. It is crucial for you to ensure that you go through all the terms to make sure that you know what you are getting into. You will be able to generate a decent income only if you spend time researching the products, and it will be worth the effort.

Here are some pointers to bear in mind.

You must look at the types of sellers who are using the network, as it will help you understand how successful the affiliation or affiliate program can be.

You must look into the network and check the type of programs and payment systems that exist.

Ideally, you must look for programs that pay you 50 to 60% commission so that you can make the most of the affiliation. If you are using a platform like Clickbank, then it can be a little higher. The basic idea is to find products and programs that are going to help you make the most of the affiliation.

If you choose a cost per action scheme, then you have to find programs that pay above $1 and ensure that the products are not too restrictive and can be promoted freely.

For any physical products that you promote, look for at least $40 and above commissions.

Before choosing any products and services, you have to ask yourself whether it goes with your image and if people will be willing to buy it. Do not endorse anything that goes against your image.

You have to analyze the sales pitch that you can use to bag the affiliate and what ideas you can use to promote the products.

It is essential to check the type of support that the program provides. You must have customer care service numbers that you can call in case you have any queries and have quick solutions to problems.

Site Building

Once you recognize your niche market and research your affiliates, you can build your site. This step is all about putting your plans into action. If you already have a website of the blog up and running, then you must work on finding your affiliates. But if you don't have one, then here are the steps to adopt.

First off, you have to decide upon a domain name and pick something that is unique to you. You must be recognizable so that people know it's your website. Many popular websites give you the chance to register your domain name, such as GoDaddy.com. Once you decide on the title, check if it is available and buy it so that you don't lose the chance of getting your desired domain name.

Once done, you have to set up the blog or website. Look for reliable hosts who give you good features to work with. Some good hosts include BlueHost and GoDaddy.com.

Next, you have to install WordPress so that you have a CMS to work with. You will be given a one-click option that you can use to install it on your site.

Next, you have to install the theme and make it unique.

Once done, you have to add the content. It is this content that will help you find your target affiliates.

Making the Content

One of the most critical steps involved in the process of affiliate marketing is creating content. The content is what draws people to your blog or website and helps with finding affiliates. Remember that content is King and it is essential to come up with some that brings value to your customer. If you need help in knowing some of the lucrative niches, then they are as follows:

Reviews

Everybody loves seeing reviews and reactions. If you wish to create a niche for yourself, then you must review products that have not yet been reviewed or be the first one to review something. You can choose any niche you like such as makeup, technology, kitchen appliances, etc. You will stand a chance of getting these sent over to you to review them.

Blogs on Current Affairs

Remember that the Internet is one of the best tools to use to find information. More and more people use the Internet to find relevant information. If you give them that information, then you can instantly catapult your popularity. People will keep coming back to your blog if they keep getting the latest news and updates. For example, if you keep updating your blog about the latest fashion trends or news about stocks, then people will keep coming back to your blog for the latest information.

Free Courses

People tend to look for places where they can get free content. This can be an eBook, dance lessons, singing lessons, language lessons, make up instructions, etc. All these happen to be niche ideas that you can use to find your target audience. You can make use of email marketing to generate leads and get more and more people to view your videos or visit your blog page. A good way of monetizing it is by incorporating the products that you wish to sell so that you can promote it effortlessly. You have to know that nobody will be interested in generic content and need something specific. Generic content leads to lesser traffic, and in turn lower sales. So you have to put in the effort of giving them value-based products that are sure to keep them coming back for more.

Building an Audience

The next task for you is to build a large audience base. The audience is what will help you get your affiliate marketing rolling. Many people assume that an audience will start building as soon as you get your blog rolling. But this is not true, as you have to put in the effort of finding an audience and retaining them. Remember that you will require a steady stream of views to maintain popularity. For this, you have to do certain things that will keep your audience interested in what you are putting out. Here are some tips to help you increase your customer base.

Social Media

Social media is all about assisting people to promote their business and grab as many eyeballs as possible. If you are not making use of social media to promote your blogs and websites, then you are missing out on almost 50% more audience. There are many different social media platforms to choose from, including Facebook, Twitter, and Instagram. You have to link all of them together so that you can make the most of their promotional capabilities. Create a Facebook page and share it with your contacts. You can ask your friends to share too so that you can increase your viewership. Link all your social media accounts so that people know you are the same person and have an online business.

Collaborations

It is essential to collaborate with others so that you can promote your channel. If there is someone who has a lot more subscribers and followers than you, then you can ask them to be a guest on your blog or videos or feature in theirs. You might have to pay them an incentive for it, but it will be well worth it as you can increase your viewership. If you happen to capitalize on even 40% of their audience, then you will successfully increase your audience base. Do as much collaboration as you can so that you can push your chances of finding a bigger audience.

Power of SEO

SEO stands for search engine optimization and using it the right way can help you increase your audience base by a large margin. When you wish to make use of search engine optimization, you have to ensure that you know what words and hashtags to use so that you can reach out to a large audience. You can make use of a tool that will give you these words that can be used to catapult your popularity and be noticed more.

Email Lists

Email marketing can help you promote your blog, website, or channel by sending regular updates. You increase chances of people clicking on your blog link if you keep sending them reminders. Remember that you have to time the emails so that they reach the audience at the right times. Early evenings are the best time to send reminders.

Paid Advertising

Some affiliate marketers engage in paid advertising to increase their traffic and drive up product sales. Paid advertising can be done through social media, as it is easier to do so. Google AdWords is a good tool to drive sales and traffic up.

Promoting Affiliates

This happens to be the most crucial part of the monetizing process. Once your blog, website or channel is on a roll, you must promote your affiliate's products and services. The basic idea is to sell to as many people as possible so that you can push sales upwards. Here are some ways in which you can promote affiliate products.

Product Reviews

One of the best ways to promote products is through product reviews. Your affiliate merchant will send products that you have to review for them. You have to add in links to the product so that those who like it can be led to the website to purchase the product. Remember that honest reviews are much better than fabricated ones. You have to build your credibility by telling people your real experiences and what they can expect from the product. Once you put in the link and your audience member buys the product, then you have made your first sale!

Ads

Banner ads have existed for a long time and are one of the most popular ways of advertising products. Affiliate marketers post banner ads on their blogs and websites so that people can click on it and be redirected to the product website. All that you have to do is place the ad on a page that has lots of traffic. This will push your sales upwards. You have to find the best page to place the banners to capitalize on the chance.

Context Links

Context links are some of the easiest ways of promoting products and services belonging to affiliates. It is where you add the links to certain aspects of your blog, such as specific words that will lead the audience to the product. For example, if you run a food-based blog then you can link ingredients to actual products that you used to prepare the recipe. Your audience will be interested in using the same ingredients and will most likely click on the link to buy. This will help you drive up sales and, in turn, your income.

Email Promotion

As mentioned earlier, using email is still a very lucrative way of capitalizing on your audience base. You can use the leads to send them product links and links to reviews. They can click on it and be redirected to the products. If you have a large following, then merely clicking on the link can help you monetize your affiliate links.

Discounts and Giveaways

Everybody loves discounts! One of the best ways to promote affiliate products is by offering your audience a unique discount that they can only get through your blog, website, or channel. You can also inform your audience about a sale that is going on at the website. Giveaways are also a big hit. You can give away the products to a lucky winner, etc.

These are the different ways in which you can promote products and it's best to choose a technique that works well. Remember that some affiliates will have rigid rules for ways in which you can promote their products. Some will only accept banner ads, while others will only accept email marketing, etc. You have to use the same to stay within promotional parameters.

Bear in mind that it is now mandatory, as per US FTC laws, to put up a disclaimer on your website or blog that says you have affiliate links with the company whose products you are promoting. This will work as a basic courtesy towards your viewers so that they know about it when they click on the links.

Repeat

The last step of the process is repeating all the above steps. You have to adopt the same measures for all the new businesses that you set up. It is important to continue what you are doing so that your audience base can be consistently expanded, and you have more businesses to fall back on.

Earn from Affiliate Marketing

One of the easiest ways in which you can make money online is by taking up affiliate marketing. You don't have to work on product ideas, product creation, providing customer support, or any other problems that are associated with the creation and development of a product. All that you need to do is promote a product.

Build Your Website Traffic First, and be Patient

Affiliate marketing thrives on people's interest in clicking on links to products that catch their eye. But who are these "people"? All those who visit your blog or website to read what you have written. So, your blog or site must be as interesting as possible, if you are interested in luring them. Remember that you need to establish a good reader base in order to land an affiliate marketing gig. Your content must be as engaging as the look of your blog or website.

If you're not getting a good number of unique visitors to your website, you're not going to get the click-through to your affiliate. Here, "unique" refers to new customers and not the same old ones who have probably bookmarked you and keep visiting all the time. The traffic to your blog or site increases when the number of people visiting it is going to increase. Not everyone is going to click on the links, and to get a reasonable number of clicks, you need plenty of regular visitors. You also need to build up a reputation as an expert in your niche before people will trust you enough to go for your recommendations. There must be interesting content for people to read and remain glued. It is not helpful if they visit just once and immediately forget about your blog. You need to track the number of people that visit your page and record the numbers per day, per month, and per year. This will help you to know how popular your blog really is.

One Good Product or Business is Enough

Now that we understood who these "people" are that will ensure good traffic comes your way, let us look at what they will be interested in.

Newcomers to the system often make the mistake of peppering their site or sites with lots of different things, imagining that people are likely to buy more because they have more choice. It is typical human thinking to want a lot of choice in anything and everything, let alone links on a website. You are not a store – you don't have to offer your customers choice, because they did not land on your site with purchase in mind. They're there for information, and if you're good at what you do, you'll be able to persuade them to buy something while they are there, so you can make some cash.

Think of it as a classy gig to have only one website promotion and that website is the best one that your readers can have. That is, you will have the chance to promote one product or service better rather than having to do it for 5 or 6 different ones. Not only will that confuse your customers, but it will confuse you as well. You will have to look into two or three different companies and think of where their links will look the best. Think of yourself as a pop-up store to promote one product as opposed to a supermarket that offers a lot of choices.

The power of suggestion works on a majority of the customers. They will take a liking to something if you tell them that you are offering them the same product that you have personally tested and liked yourself.

Don't make the mistake of putting up too many choices at once. If you have put up just one product and the website is offering it at the best price in the market, then even if the person has left your site to do a quick price comparison, he or she is sure to return to yours to click on the ad. Also, focusing on a single product or business makes it easier to make keywords work for you. So, stick with one business or product. If you want to do more, set up a different website for each affiliate, and concentrate on that, rather than spreading yourself too thinly. What you can then do is link your sites.

Content is Very Important

This is true of any website, of course, but it's especially relevant if you are hoping to make money from affiliate marketing. People go to websites to be informed or entertained – often both at the same time. So, make sure you have plenty of content structured around the products or business you are promoting.

Another point to remember is that search engines can tell whether there's quality content on your site, and will rank it higher as a result. That means more visitors and hopefully more sales. You must be well versed with the concept of "SEO." SEO refers to search engine optimization. You must have heard that many companies have a good SEO team that helps them become popular. Well, this is true because these teams will work hard on promoting the websites and blogs of the company and help it appear at the top of the Google search list.

You must pick out all the top words from your blog or website, that are most likely going to be typed by people. If they get the combination of words right, then your site is going to appear as the topmost links. For this, you can also make use of a small description that will help you put in all the main words.

But remember just a good SEO description will not do the trick and you need to have good content as well. So, forget about the keyword-stuffed sales pitches when you are coming up with content for your blog – educate, inform, entertain, but whatever you do, don't spam. You don't need long articles – in fact, three hundred-word posts will hold the attention of your audience better than one 800 to 900-word post. The more information you give away, the better the reader base. Most people will look for sites that give them an in-depth look at difficult topics. By making it easy for them, you will have a chance to increase your reader base.

You need to be as different and unique as possible. For instance, if you wish to provide customers with recipe ideas then come up with good and unique ones that are not easily available on the Internet. Once they take a liking to your unique recipes, they will be interested in clicking on an ad in your site, which might be a particular cream cheese brand, or even baking trays. You can also explicitly mention that you have used these brands and hyperlink the products with the words. Your readers are sure to click on them!

Keep the posts on the topic, and plant the idea in the reader's mind that they need to buy whatever you're promoting. You can even drop a contextual link to a particular product. Help them reach a decision, rather than trying to direct them straight to the sales site. The soft approach is the best approach here as you are trying to be subtle about your promoting. I am sure you yourself have bought many things by clicking on ads put up on blogs and sites that you read.

Promote Your Site

This sounds obvious, but if you want people to come to your site, read your content, and click on your affiliate links, you need to let them know the site exists. Whether it is a product or a service, everything needs to be promoted for people to be aware of what you are doing. Without proper promotion, how are you going to get word about your website out there? There are only so many friends that will click on your links, and in order for you to land a big gig, you will need at least 1000 clicks a week.

Firstly, list your site in search engines, write press releases to be distributed online, and promote your site on forums in your niche and social media.

If you have a friend whose blog is extremely popular then you can consider asking him or her to subtly promote yours on theirs. But you might have to consider paying them a small fee for it, as you will be benefitting from their service to you. If you don't have any such friends, but know of someone who has such a blog, then you can consider contacting them and asking them politely to promote yours. It's a good idea to have Facebook and Twitter accounts linked to your website, and set up so that each time you post an update on the site it's posted to your social media account. You can also have a Facebook page dedicated to your website or blog where you will keep updating links to your site. Work on building an army of followers, but don't even consider buying them. Bought followers are not going to go to your website and click on the affiliate links – they just give a false illusion that your social media account is more popular than it really is. You might think of being popular, but once the bubble bursts, you might be extremely disappointed. If it is a group of friends, then make sure the group is genuinely interested in your blog or site and are not doing you a favor. Those will only last for a while and decide to abandon you once they lose interest.

Don't be Invisible or Anonymous

This is a golden rule. First and foremost, you have to have confidence in who you are and what you do. If you don't have self-confidence, then it will not work in your favor. Just because it's easy to hide behind an alias on the Internet, it doesn't mean you should. It can be tempting to use a cool name but don't do it. If you want to build credibility and earn money online, you have to be seen as a real person, with proper contact details. Don't hide behind a pen name or a nickname, use a real name and an email address tied to your domain name, rather than a Hotmail or an AOL account. If you wish to use a pen name, then consider putting it in brackets so that the person is aware of your real name as well. Make sure you write out your full name including initials, as there can be many others with the same name as you. Remember that people need to know they can contact you with questions and that they will get an answer from a real person. They might also ask for a genuine photograph, just to be sure of who the other person is. If they can't trust the Webmaster, they're not going to click on the affiliate link and you won't make any money. It's all about trustworthiness.

Before you start to make money from affiliate marketing, you need to have your site set up to encourage people to click through on the advertising links. That means having great content that's informative and/or entertaining, earning a reputation for being an expert in your niche and taking a soft approach to selling. Let your knowledge and enthusiasm persuade the reader to click through, rather than filling the site with banners and sales pitches. Also, be sure to provide proper contact details so your readers know you are a real person. Now you're ready to sell, but what are the best affiliate products to sell, and how can you get started?

Chapter Seven: Creation of Digital/Informational Product

There is a huge market for online courses and they have great potential. Did you know that online learning was valued at over $165 billion in 2015? Well, that's a lot of money, isn't it? In this section, you will learn about the different steps that you can follow to create an online course and earn money from it.

Step 1: Commitment

You need to commit yourself to create a course. Since you are reading this, it is apparent that you want to create an online course. Online courses are here to stay, and they have great potential. Graham Cochran teaches music production online, and he makes around $75,000 a month! Success is excellent, regardless of how big or small it is. For instance, it would be nice to earn even $500 or $1000 from your course every month! If you want to make money, then you need to put in some effort. After all, there is no such thing as "100%" passive income. You must create the course once, and after that, you can get paid repeatedly. You can sell the course over the years if it is still relevant. If you want to create an online course, that's good! You don't have to be an expert if you're going to create a class. There are two options if you want to create a course. The first option is to be the expert and the second one is to be a curious beginner. If you are already an expert on a topic, then it can be quite easy to share your knowledge with others. You might be a certified therapist, masseuse, or something else. So, why don't you share your experience with the world? The other option is to learn as you create a course. Let us be honest now, not every one of us is an expert. However, if you want to learn and have a thirst for knowledge, then you can create a course too. Select a topic that interests you and learn about it as much as you can. Once you do this, you can create a class. When you learn, you must document the process, and you can create a course on anything. You can even create a course on building courses! You can create an app on how to write, and so on. Knowledge is a beautiful thing to possess, and the more knowledgeable you are about a subject, the better you will be at it.

Step 2: Idea

Now that you know that you want to create a course, you need to select an idea. Not just any idea, an idea that is profitable. You can either create a class about something that you know or something that you are learning. How do you select an idea? Not just that, how can you make sure that the idea you choose is a profitable one? It isn't nice to spend a lot of your time creating a course that has no takers in the end. In fact, this is one of the biggest mistakes a lot of new course makers commit. If you notice that someone else has already created a course like the one you have in mind, it is a good thing! It might sound counterintuitive, but bear with me. When you come up with an idea that no one has ever tried before, it can mean two things. It can either imply that your idea is exceptionally innovative or that no one is probably interested in that idea. To be honest, neither of these things is any good. The Internet is a massive network, and you will find takers for almost anything. However, at times you might not, and you must understand this. As a beginner, three simple strategies will help you to select an idea. Take stock of all those things that others tend to ask you questions or your advice about. Find a problem that people face, and you can try to address that problem, but this involves a lot of research. The third option is quite simple. Everyone has issues, and if you talk to your friends or family members about the things they need help with, you can find an idea that will work well for you.

Step 3: Test the Idea

You must test your idea to see if it has any potential. It is disappointing to create a course and not find any takers for it. You can either create a free brief email-course or you can pre-sell your course. You can email the mini course to your colleagues, friends, acquaintances, and family members, and ask for their feedback. You can even pre-sell the course before you create it. It will enable you to know about all those who are interested in the course you create. Both these strategies will help you to test the viability of your idea.

Step 4: Create an Outline

Now that you know that your idea is viable, the next step is to create the course outline. There is a lot of content that you must design, and you need to make sure that the content you offer is top-notch. You need a clear course outline. You don't have to create an in-depth course that includes everything you can think of. You must start small, and you can expand from there. Prioritize the content you want to add. Think of the problem that your course addresses and list the steps that someone must follow to achieve their goal. Now that you know the steps, you can break your course down into small lessons. If you want to create a class about dating, the first lesson can be to overcome the fear of flirting; the next will be to get someone's attention, and so on. Each lesson will get the viewer a step closer to their goal. Don't try to pack all the content into one lesson. That is too much information for the viewer. Make sure that a single lesson doesn't exceed 10 minutes.

Step 5: Course Content

Most courses are given in a video format. You must include a couple of worksheets that the student can use to implement all that they learn. It is okay even if your first course doesn't look that great. It is okay if your content is good. It is good to compare your course to other online courses. But don't try to be a perfectionist. You can start with a whiteboard and a chair, and it is okay. You can improve your course when you start to gain some experience. After all, even you are learning how to create a class. Don't fuss too much about the quality of production. Instead, your primary focus must be on the content you deliver. If you provide practical tips and easy to follow step-by-step instructions, you can gain more students. The most popular form of online course is video. However, you can opt for audio, text, video, or a combination of these three styles. You can edit and shoot the videos on your own. If the lighting is excellent, and the audio is clear, you are good to go. If you provide worksheets, they must always be in the form of a PDF. PDF files are easy to download and print.

Go Online

Now that you have an idea and useful content, the next step is to get your course online. If you don't get your course online, how will you sell it? There are different sites that you can use to upload your course to. You can use a platform like Zippy or Udemy to offer your classes to your audience. The other option is to create a course site for yourself. If you have the ownership of your course site, you can control all the aspects of the course, and you don't have to share your revenue with anyone else. Now that your course is online, you must decide a price for it. Go through other online courses that address the same issue as yours, and you can price your course accordingly. Price it low, at least initially. Once you find a good audience base for yourself, you can slowly increase the price. Well, now that your course is up and running, the next step is to create viewership for yourself.